Rex Milligan R

Other books by Anthony Buckeridge in Armada

Rex Milligan's Busy Term
Rex Milligan Holds Forth
Rex Milligan Reporting
According to Jennings
Jennings Goes to School
Jennings' Little Hut
The Trouble with Jennings
Jennings and Darbishire
Trust Jennings
Jennings, as Usual
Jennings' Diary

Rex Milligan Raises the Roof

Anthony Buckeridge

For B.M.L.

First published in the U.K. in 1955 by Lutterworth Press Limited.
This edition was first published by
William Collins Sons & Co. Ltd., 14 St. James's Place, London S.W.1, in 1973.

Printed in Great Britain by
Love & Malcomson Ltd., Brighton Road, Redhill, Surrey.

THE CALL TO ARMS

THERE isn't much to do on the last day of the summer holidays—apart from oiling your cricket bat and having your hair cut. So when the Secondary Technical School challenged us to a mock battle on the patch of waste ground behind the gasworks, we felt it was just what we needed to liven up a dull half hour.

Ever since I've been at Sheldrake Grammar our juniors have been in a state of open warfare with the Tech in Spencer Road. Nothing serious, mind you; in fact it's a rather friendly business as feuds go, and nobody gets hurt as we've worked out a list of combat rules to stop people from going berserk and acting like dangerous maniacs.

All the same, the battles are quite hectic while they last. Both sides mobilize an armoured column made up of soap-boxes on wheels and self-propelled perambulators; and you need to keep your eye on these vehicles, believe me, because they carry a heavy bomb-load of brown paper bags filled with wet sawdust.

Then there are the infantry units. These vary a bit, depending on how many chaps happen to be milling around, anxious to join the fray; but as a rule we can usually muster a dozen or so hand-picked commandos who charge into battle armed with garden syringes for long-range squirting, and captive football bladders for zonking opponents over the head at close quarters.

The object of each skirmish is to capture ye flag of ye foe, while at the same time defending your own tattered relic down to the last inky-fingered fourth-former.

There's not much left of the Sheldrake flag now, I'm afraid. It started life as a bath towel, belonging to my friend Jigger Johnson, but what with a certain amount of rough handling in the heat of many battles it looks like some historic banner preserved since the Wars of the Roses.

The Tech's dog-eared remnant of bunting isn't in much better shape, either. However, we don't worry about little things like that, because the battles of the flags serve as a good excuse for a spot of friendly rough-housing, whenever one side thinks the other is getting too big for its boots, and needs taking down a couple of lace-holes.

Naturally, you'd expect to find a certain amount of rivalry between two large day schools in the same suburb, and we're no exception in the way we try to outshine our opposite numbers. But it doesn't stop at that: feeling runs high and sometimes the cross-fire of competition grows hot enough to blister the paint.

Don't ask me why! It's just the way things are; though perhaps one reason why the fur flies so furiously is that each school is so very different from the other.

Take the buildings, for instance. The Secondary Tech have got modern premises, so plastered with up-to-date gadgets that they look more like a space-ship terminus than a seat of learning. Outside, it's all vita glass and gleaming white concrete; and as soon as you step through the door you find yourself traipsing along soundproof corridors, and breathing lungfuls of guaranteed Grade *A* atmosphere which filters in through their air-conditioning plant.

The whole place is as bright as technicolor, and

fitted with the latest thing in chromium-plated desk legs. So what with one thing and another, the chaps at the Tech rather pride themselves on their plastic palace, and tend to look down their noses at the happy-go-lucky architecture of Sheldrake's.

And not without reason! You see, the Grammar School is a very old foundation; so old that parts of the building don't seem to have got much foundation left, if you follow me.

There's no chromium plating about our fittings, for instance. Our classrooms are decorated with match-boarding and chocolate paint instead of the three shades of yellow affected by the Tech. . . . And all we know about air-conditioning in Form 4 classroom, is that we have to keep the window open to avoid being suffocated by the fumes from the boiler in the basement. Mind you, we *have* got a couple of modern classroom blocks with central heating of sorts, but we don't swank about it. We prefer to pride ourselves on our ancient venerable traditions, rather than up-to-date premises.

Well, that's enough, for the moment, about the architectural lay-out; so let's go back to the last day of the holidays.

My friend Jigger Johnson is Officer-in-Charge of the Grammar Commandos, and when he received the challenge from Spikey Andrews, the leader of the Tech Brigade, he lost no time in rounding up a bevy of Sheldrake fourth-formers and roping them in for the fray. We sketched out our plan of campaign at a staff officers' meeting in Jigger's tool shed on the morning of the battle.

"We'll kick off with a diversion in strength on their left flank," Jigger decided. "As soon as they move over to check it, we'll launch a frontal assault with first line tanks to open up a gap for our infantry. I shall want everyone at action stations, ready to move off, at 13.15 hours."

"What time's that?" queried Alfie Cutforth. Maths isn't his strong point.

"Quarter past one, you coot," Jigger translated. "Spikey wants the *Cease Fire* at quarter to two. The Tech went back to school yesterday, so the whole operation has got to be carried out during their dinner hour. . . . Any questions?"

"Yes, what I'd like to know . . ." Alfie began.

"I don't mean *silly* questions," Jigger pointed out curtly; and as Alfie has never been known to ask anything else, he tailed off into silence after catching a warning look from the Officer-in-Charge.

You'd like Jigger Johnson: he's a stocky, square-rigged sort of chap with red hair and freckles. He and I have been friends ever since we scrambled through our Grammar School entrance exam together, and we've kept pace ever since. We've both reached the ripe old age of 13-*plus* without getting on each other's nerves, so it's fairly safe to say that the friendship of Messrs. R. Milligan and J. Johnson has withstood the test of time, and is something you can count on in this uncertain world.

Anyway, no one seemed to have any more questions, so I caught the Speaker's eye and put forward a bright scheme which had been percolating through my so-called brain for the past few minutes.

"Listen, Jig," I said. "The Tech had things pretty well all their own way last time; and if we're going to turn the tables today, we shall need a craftier scheme than our usual method of bashing through by brute force and trusting to luck. So I vote we spring a fast one on them, and drop a couple of airborne parachutists behind the enemy lines, while Spikey and Co. are looking the other way."

There was a puzzled silence while my fellow staff-officers looked at me as though I'd just dropped in from Cloud-cuckoo-land.

Then up spake a worthy type called Boko Phipps.

"Don't be so stark raving- crackers, Rex!" he said. "All very well to talk about parachutists, but what do we use for aircraft?"

So I explained my water-tight wheeze in simple words which even Alfie Cutforth could understand.

There are two trees on the waste ground—sorry, on the *theatre of operations*, I should say—a short distance behind the tumbledown shed where the Tech Brigade display their flag and muster their forces for action. There's no other cover on this side of the battlefield, which explains why we have never been able to creep up and surprise them from the rear.

Now, my idea was to conceal a couple of chaps up the trees well before the advertised time of kick-off—say, about one o'clock, when the Tech would still be wolfing their dinners.

"All right, then: zero hour strikes," I went on. "The infantry, tanks and all supporting troops start blazing away; and when the hurly-burly is at its height, our secret tree-squatters descend to earth. Then they advance on the shed from the only direction which is sure to be unguarded, and snaffle the Tech's flag before the enemy can get back to base."

"But what happens to our airborne personnel after that?" objected Boko. "They won't have a hope of getting back to their own lines."

"That's where the tanks come in," I told him. "Only, instead of trying to knock Spike's forces for six, they'll have to defend a narrow corridor, so that our parachutists can beetle along it at full tilt with the enemy banner in tow."

"It might work," Jigger conceded. "It's about time we tried something new. The Tech will be getting somewhat uppish if we don't take them down a peg pretty soon."

Grunts of agreement rose up on all sides. We'd come off second best in our last encounter, and though we hadn't actually lost our flag it had been a very near thing.

What had really caught us napping was the Tech Brigade's secret weapon—a stirrup-pump which Spikey Andrews had scrounged from goodness knows where and mounted on an armoured soap-box. According to the rules he was entitled to claim a casualty for every one of our chaps who got splashed; and before you could say "Fossilized fish-hooks" he'd had our raiding party in his nozzle-sights and was squirting them down like greenfly. That meant that all our casualties had to stand by for the rest of the battle, as useless as a bunch of burst balloons. And we didn't want *that* happening again!

"Righto, then. We'll try Rex's scheme and hope for the best," Jigger decided.

"Oh wacko!" crowed Alfie Cutforth. "Clear the runway for the Sheldrake Airborne unit. Look out, Sound Barrier, here I come!"

Then he charged round the tool shed in small circles, spluttering and gargling at full throttle to give us his famous imitation of a jet aircraft bursting through the supersonic barrier.

"Pipe down, Cutforth. You're not likely to be picked for the job, anyway," said Boko. Which was only too true.

Alfie talks a lot, but when it comes to a rough-house

he's jolly careful to keep well away from the target area. Officially he's our signals officer, but as he's about as much use as an Eskimo's sunshade, we let him spend most of his time helping Staggers in the Secret Weapons department.

Do you remember the Staggers?—J. O. Stagg, to give him his full title. He's our bulging-browed wonderman of science with a flair for inventing unworkable gadgets. His latest contribution to our commando equipment was a field telephone consisting of a pair of earphones made out of cocoa-tin lids, and connected, *via* a long piece of elastic, to a morse-buzzer.

Wherever the fighting is thinnest you'll find Alfie Cutforth prancing round in the earphones, with Stagg trailing after him buzzing away like a plague of bluebottles. So far no message has ever been known to get through, because Alfie has to take the earphones off to hear what Stagg is woffling about. Still, it keeps them happy!

Well, the upshot of my famous brainwave was that Boko Phipps and I were detailed for the airborne assignment. I was pleased about that because Boko's got his head screwed on the right way. To look at him you wouldn't think he had the brains of a newt, yet he always comes top of the form without exerting himself in the slightest degree. My only doubt was whether he'd be able to run fast enough if we found ourselves in a tight corner. He's a good type, is B. Phipps, but he's no four-minute miler.

"You'll have to work out the drill as you go along," Jigger told us. "I suggest you both bale out of your trees at a given signal; and if one of you gets nabbed it'll be up to the other to carry on by himself. . . . Okay then, chaps, that's all for now."

I met Boko on the waste ground at one o'clock, according to schedule. He was clutching a little cardboard box in one hand, and a jam jar of water in the other.

"I've got something here that might come in handy," he greeted me. "I bought it at the toy shop on the corner." And from the box he produced a flimsy object which looked like a penny whistle with a metal ball screwed on the end.

"It's a bird-warbler," he explained proudly. "You fill the ball with water, blow down the pipe, and it makes a noise like a nightingale. Satisfaction guaranteed or money back. As demonstrated on television!"

"You're off your rocker," I told him severely. "We've been picked for an important airborne mission. We shan't have time to flit from branch to branch warbling like a brace of nightingales."

"You don't understand. It's for signalling in code," he said. "I shan't be able to shout across to you with the Tech Brigade milling about just beneath us—they'd spot us in a flash. But nobody's going to pay much attention to a little birdie singing its heart out in the tree-tops. It goes like this, look."

He filled the ball with water from his jam jar, and blew down the spout by way of demonstration. Sure enough, a high-pitched trilling noise broke on the air.

"Good, isn't it?" crowed Boko triumphantly. "You can see now why the poet Keats was so fond of writing odes about twitterings of this type."

There was something to be said for Boko's idea—or the Phipps Plan, as he insisted on calling it. I knew I shouldn't be able to see very well from my tree because the tumble-down shed blocked my line of vision. But Boko's perch would give him a bird's-eye view of the whole area, so a pre-arranged warble would be a good way of letting me know when the coast was clear.

"One long trill means, 'Now's our chance—let's get cracking'. Short jerky notes mean, 'Danger: enemy guarding hut'," Boko explained, fixing the top on to his jam jar and easing it into his pocket. Whereupon, we scrambled up our respective trees for a quick rehearsal.

I couldn't see Boko nestling amongst the foliage with his jam jar, but his signals came over loud and clear; and what's more they really *did* sound like a nightingale. We had a little time in hand, so while he practised his chirruping I sat astride a branch and let my eye roam round the scenery.

I shan't take up much time in describing the grandeur of the landscape, because two gas-holders and a railway siding were about the only things on the horizon. But then, our suburb is so built up that it's like that almost everywhere you look.

The only human being in sight was a tall, elderly character in a hairy tweed suit and a cloth cap, mooching along a little path which crossed the waste ground. He walked with a slight stoop and peered vaguely over the tops of his gold-rimmed bi-focals as though his mind was miles away.

Soon he drew level with my perch, about ten yards away on the port beam. Then, suddenly, he came to a dead stop, swivelled round like a rotating gun-turret and looked hard at Boko's tree.

"Tweet-tweet-tweet! Chirrup, chirrup, chirrup!" warbled Boko happily.

The old boy's vagueness vanished in a flash and he trotted up to the tree, scanning the branches keenly for a close-up of the feathered songster.

In this, he was unlucky. Boko kept himself well out

of focus, while continuing to trill and chirrup like the front row of the dawn chorus.

The elderly bird-watcher stared goggle-eyed in bewilderment. Then he took a diary from his pocket, glanced at his watch and started to make notes. You couldn't blame him for getting so excited; after all, you don't often hear nightingales singing behind gas works in busy London suburbs during the dinner hour.

As it happened, it didn't sing for long, because a few moments later Spikey Andrews and the Tech Brigade came trundling their armoured soap-boxes and makeshift weapons along to battle stations, and making as much noise about it as a brass foundry working overtime.

The bird-watcher turned to them with imploring gestures of silence.

"Ssh! Ssh! Quiet please, quiet," he pleaded. "I've just observed a remarkable thing—a nightingale singing in broad daylight; and in London, too. Tread softly and you can hear it for yourselves."

His tone was so urgent that Spikey and Co. *did* stop and listen, from sheer surprise. Then they all clustered round Boko's tree, gawping up into the branches with their ears pretty well out on strings, as per instructions.

Boko couldn't resist the temptation. He tipped the jam jar of water upside down through a gap in the foliage, and scored a direct hit on Spikey Andrews' upturned face.

Spikey leapt like a startled stag, and swung round angrily upon the inoffensive bird-watcher.

"Is that your idea of a joke?" he spluttered, mopping his streaming face with an off-white handkerchief. "I didn't think people of your age went about setting booby traps for strangers."

The naturalist stared at him thunderstruck.

"Good heavens! How did that happen? I had no idea . . . Surely you don't hold *me* responsible. I was merely drawing your attention to the song of the nightingale."

"*Cuckoo* would have been nearer the mark," Spikey retorted with bad grace; and it was obvious that he wasn't too pleased at being made to look foolish in front of his troops. This didn't surprise me, because friend Andrews can be an awkward character to deal with when anything upsets him.

I'm not saying a word against him, mind you. So far as I know, he's big-hearted, loyal, generous and overflowing with virtue and good works. All I *will* say is, that if he's on one side and you're on the other, it pays to keep your eye on him, you mark my words!

Ronald (Spikey) Andrews earned his position as leader of the Technical School Expeditionary Force by proving himself to be bolder and craftier than any of his colleagues. He's a few months older than I am; tall for his age and rather on the scraggy side, with a pale face and pointed features. He's got straight, straw-coloured hair which hangs down over his eyebrows like a fringe on an Old English sheepdog.

At the moment, his pale features were flushed with righteous indignation, and it looked as though he wasn't going to be satisfied until he'd discovered what the unexpected showerbath was in aid of.

"I don't get this. What have you got up that tree?" he demanded suspiciously.

"My dear boy, you mistake my intentions, I assure you. I am completely nonplussed by this unexpected turn of events!" The old boy shook his head in bemused wonder, quite unable to cope with the situation.

"Funny way for a nightingale to behave. I'm going

up to have a squint at close quarters," Spikey decided, reaching out for one of the lower branches.

I felt anxious. It was all very well for Boko to indulge in monkey business with jam pots, but if it meant our famous scheme was going to be nipped in the bud, the joke wouldn't be so funny after all.

Fortunately, our Grammar School armoured column appeared on the skyline just then, all set to launch the attack. Spikey caught sight of them out of the corner of his eye.

"Come on, chaps! Action stations!" he yelled, abandoning his quest for rare birds: and in two shakes of a lamb's tail the Tech personnel had beetled off at the double, leaving a very bewildered naturalist wondering whether he was on his head or his heels. He shook his head in a puzzled sort of way and wandered off towards the gas works.

As things turned out, we hadn't seen the last of our vague character in hairy tweeds and bi-focal spectacles. But at that moment I was too busy to bother about him, because the opposing forces were already lining up for the start of the battle.

Then a distant clock chimed the quarter. . . . Zero hour had arrived.

PRISONER IN CHAINS

THE next best thing to being in the thick of a battle is to watch it from the top of a tree. I couldn't follow all the hurly-burly, of course, as the Tech's tumbledown shed cut off my line of vision in one direction. But to begin with, most of the action took place on my side of the battle-field, where the waste ground slopes down sharply on three sides to form a little crater at the bottom.

The general idea is to send the so-called tanks thundering *whoosh-bang-slap* down one slope, and then to man-handle them up the other, to attack the enemy camp at the top. Of course, it seldom works out as scheduled: most of the wheeled soap-boxes are certain to stop a wet sawdust bomb before they're anywhere near their objective.

The alternative is for the rickety chariots to get up speed going down the slope and cannon into their opposite number at the bottom. A broadside hit counts as a victory for the attacker, while a head-on collision automatically knocks out both the vehicles involved.

Going into action on foot with the anti-tank squad is no rest-cure either; because if you want to knock out an enemy vehicle when you're unmounted, you have to crawl close enough to shove a length of stick between the spokes of its wheels as it goes past. It takes a bit of doing, believe me, but it's quite effective: if the tank happens to be moving fast at the time, it brings it to a stop with a jolt and sends the crew flying head over heels into the surrounding scenery.

Well, Jigger Johnson's tank assault got off the mark at a cracking pace. His mobile soap-boxes ploughed through the enemy's outer defences with a force that sent their anti-tank squad scurrying into their foxholes for safety.

It was first blow to us: but Spikey Andrews counter-attacked at once, sending his self-propelled perambulators skidding down the opposite slope to put a stop to any further monkey business.

In a matter of minutes, the armoured columns on both sides were looking the worse for wear. Paper-bag bombs were bursting left, right and centre; and as soon as the ammo was exhausted the tank crew jumped out of their vehicles and engaged in hand-to-hand combat.

Then the Sheldrake infantry advanced, squirting their garden syringes at full pressure, and trying to take cover from the enemy's counter-attack at the same time. The skirmishing rules are pretty rigid about this part of the drill: anyone who gets in the way of a jet of water becomes a casualty and has to stay where he is until one of his own side drags him back to base.

Now, Alfie Cutforth and Stagg had been given the job of watching the trees where Boko and I were hiding. Directly we baled out for action, they were to send a signal to Jigger in the front line, so that he could open up our escape corridor and hold the enemy back just long enough for us to get through. That was the theory, anyway: in practice it didn't work out like that at all.

To start with, there was such a racket going on all round us that Boko could have blown down his bird-warbler till he was black in the face without my hearing a single squawk. That meant I had to guess when the coast was clear; so after giving Jigger a few minutes to get organized I waved an arm to Stagg, a hundred yards away, as a sign that I was going into action.

Sizzling with efficiency, the Staggers started tapping on his morse-buzzer to the ear-phoned Alfie Cutforth at the other end of the elastic telephone wire. I don't suppose any sound reached Alfie, but he knew what was expected of him; and, absent-mindedly forgetting to remove his earphones he belted off into the fray to deliver the message.

By the time he had run ten yards the elastic was

stretched to breaking point. The next second the transmitter was whisked out of the Stagger's grasp, and shot through the intervening space like a guided missile to finish up with a resounding *plonk* on Alfie's tin-lidded ear.

I laughed so much I nearly fell out of my tree. But I couldn't afford to make merry at Alfie's expense, because by this time Boko had already made a perfect three-point landing and was legging it towards the tumbledown hut as fast as his size eight juvenile footwear would carry him.

I slithered off my branch and scrambled down after him; but just as I was jumping the last few feet down to ground level, I heard a shout away to my left.

"Hey! Watch out. There's two of them, look! Sneaking up from the rear. After them quick!"

It was one of Spikey's corporals who had spotted us—a podgy youth of thirteen with outsized ears and rabbity teeth. I knew him slightly: his proper name was Tucker, but for some unknown reason he always answered to the nickname of Bubblegum.

"Round 'em up! They're making a break for our flag," he yelled. Whereupon a dozen of the Tech's supporting troops broke away from the main battlefront and came charging back to base to cope with the new assault in their rear.

The odds were too heavy against us. Boko went down like a pole-axed ox as three of the enemy hurled themselves on him in a triple rugger tackle. I was just behind him, and I had to brake hard to avoid the shemozzle of wildly kicking legs.

As I swerved to starboard, I saw Bubblegum bearing down on me with a football pump poised at the ready. He shot home the plunger, and a stream of water caught me in the chest.

"Got you!" he yelled in triumph. "Hands up! You're a casualty! I'm taking you prisoner."

"Fair enough," I agreed, when I'd got my breath back. Mind you, I was somewhat peeved about my famous plan coming unstuck at the seams; but obviously I couldn't go on fighting until I'd been liberated by one of our raiding parties.

Bubblegum Tucker came lolloping up to take charge, his ears flapping like the sails of a yacht. He was carrying one of those chains and padlocks that most of us use to prevent our bikes from being stolen.

"Hold out your wrist, Milligan," he ordered. "I'm going to make sure that you don't get liberated."

I didn't argue, because the rule says that prisoners must do as they're told. It's the only way to prevent chaos behind the lines, and it's the same for both sides, anyway.

But Bubblegum had worked out a new dodge that we'd never tried before. He wound the chain first round my wrist and then round his own.

"Little idea of mine to stop you escaping," he grinned toothily, as the self-locking padlock clicked shut. "Everywhere I go, you'll have to come too."

He never spoke a truer word: though at the time he didn't realize just what he was letting us both in for.

It seemed that Bubblegum's main job, apart from looking after prisoners, was to run around with a large enamel basin full of water, so that his front line troops had plenty of ammunition for their syringes and old bicycle pumps. It was the sort of task that needed two free hands; and after I'd managed to upset the basin a couple of times, he began to wish he hadn't got to cart me around everywhere we went.

"Mind out, you clumsy bazooka," he moaned as I

"accidentally" jerked his arm and sent half a gallon of water up his sleeve.

"Terribly sorry," I apologized, lurching against him and spilling what was left of the water over his feet. "It's your fault for chaining us together. This Siamese Twins stunt was your own idea, you know."

Somehow or other, Jigger got wind of the fact that our plan had miscarried, and that his airborne troops were prisoners in enemy hands. That meant, of course, that he had to revise his own tactics at short notice, as there was no point in holding open an escape corridor if neither Boko nor I could make use of it.

He's an adventurous type, is Jigger, so he decided to have a shot at operation Rescue—which was a pretty risky enterprise, all things considered.

I don't know how he foxed through the enemy lines without coming a cropper, but he managed it somehow; and the first inkling I had of this change of programme was the sight of Jig's freckled face weaving its way through a tuft of undergrowth, about ten yards away on my left. He was wearing sprigs of foliage on his head as a camouflage net, and fortunately Bubblegum didn't spot his stealthy approach. Nearer and nearer he crept and I was all on edge in case my podgy captor should look round and see the menace in his rear.

Out of the corner of my eye I watched the bunch of leaves crawl closer. Then, in a flash, Jigger's red head burst through the natural vegetation; an arm shot out, and a football bladder on a piece of string hurtled through space and clonked Bubblegum well and truly on the side of the head.

"Casualty! Come on, Rex, you're free," crowed Jigger, touching me on the arm as a sign that I'd been liberated.

Then he saw the chain round our wrists.

"Oh, gosh, you *can't* come, can you!"

"I jolly well can: and what's more we'll take this gruesome Tucker specimen along with us. He can be *our* prisoner for a change."

At that, I stooped down and hoisted the protesting Bubblegum on to my shoulder in a sort of fireman's lift. The chain hampered my movements, and it wasn't exactly comfortable for either of us; but we'd no time to worry about little things like that.

As it happened, I found it an advantage having Bubblegum's portly eight stone draped round me. We came under fire on our way back to the Sheldrake base, and more than once a jet of water aimed at me was conveniently warded off by the corpulent shield I was carrying.

Well, what with one thing and another, Jigger and I had rather lost track of how the battle was raging in other parts of the field; and as we staggered back into our own lines, Alfie Cutforth came prancing up, his eyes popping with shock and his cheeks wobbling with woe.

"They're breaking through on our right flank!" he twittered. "We haven't a hope of stopping the rush."

"I'll go and have a look. You'll have to stay here, I'm afraid, Rex," Jigger said.

He charged off towards the break-through, but he hadn't gone the length of a cricket pitch when a loud yell of triumph rose from the Tech's forces on our flank.

"Whacko! We've won! We've got their flag!" And there was Spikey Andrews flourishing our dog-eared banner round his head. A moment later, he was safely back inside his own territory clutching the trophy tightly and enjoying the hearty back-slapping of his supporting troops.

Jigger skidded to a halt, and turned to face me with a rueful smile.

"That's that, I'm afraid! There's nothing we can do about it at the moment: it's just time for the Cease Fire."

The church clock struck the quarter-to as he finished speaking; which meant the the skirmish was officially over. One more victory for the Tech! Things were in a pretty bad way!

Our Sheldrake troops were in no particular hurry to get away as we had a free afternoon before us: but the Tech had to be in school by two o'clock, so they started charging off the waste ground without more ado.

Not so Bubblegum!

"I'll let you go now, Milligan," he said fumbling in his pocket with his free hand for the padlock key. . . . At once a look of alarm and despondency spread over his rabbity features.

"Petrified paint-pots!" he gasped in horror. "There's a hole in my pocket—the key's gone."

I stared at him.

"Are you trying to tell me that we shall have to go about handcuffed together like this until we can file through the chain?"

"It's worse than that," he gulped in despair. "I've got to be in class in a few minutes. Old Snorker's taking our form first lesson, and I daren't be late."

"And what about me?" I queried.

"You'll have to come, too, I'm afraid," he said miserably. "There's nothing else we can do, is there?"

CUCKOO IN THE NEST

BUBBLEGUM TUCKER was one of those chaps who are quite likeable at a distance—the further off they are, the better you like them. But with that length of chain clasped firmly round our wrists, it looked as though we'd have to stick together until further notice.

"You great, addle-pated clodpoll," I stormed at him. "I've met some crazy lunatics in my time, but I reckon you take the gold medal for beetle-headedness against all comers. What did you want to go and lose the key for?"

"I didn't *want* to lose it. It was just an accidental bish," he defended himself. "Please be decent and come along to school with me, Milligan. We'll just have time to borrow a hacksaw from the carpenter's shop, if we go at once. I daren't be late because its Geography with Old Snorker, and he'll be in a gruesome bate if I march in after the lesson's started."

I began to feel sorry for Bubblegum. I had never met this Snorker character of whom he spoke so highly; but if he was anything like our Mr. Birkinshaw at the Grammar, I knew the lad would find himself batting on a sticky wicket if I didn't do something to help him.

"All right, then," I agreed. "I'll come with you as far as the carpenter's shop; but from now on you take orders from me."

"Coo, thanks," he burbled. "Let's get mobile then; there isn't a second to lose."

By this time the rest of the Tech Brigade were mere dots on the skyline, all pelting schoolwards as fast as they could run.

"We'll soon catch them up. I've got my bike behind the shed," said Bubblegum, jerking his free hand towards the Tech's front line H.Q.

"A fat lot of good your bike will be," I retorted. "Unless, by some lucky chance, it happens to be fitted with two saddles, side by side."

"Oh fish-hooks! I hadn't thought of that," he moaned. "It looks as though you'll have to run along beside me."

Was this Tucker specimen off his rocker, I wondered?

"Don't you believe it! *You're* the one that's going to do the foot-slogging. I shall be in the saddle," I told him. "And if you don't like it I shall stage a sit-down strike, and then you *will* be in the cart."

Bubblegum was beaten and he knew it. "Right-o, Milligan," he mumbled.

We retrieved the bike from behind the tumbledown shed, and with some difficulty I mounted. Then we started off.

There wasn't much slack in the chain holding our wrists together, which meant that Tucker had to trot along on the offside with his left hand held out at handlebar level. All went well till I stepped up the pace to a brisk twelve m.p.h.

"Hey! Not so fast. I can't keep up," he panted.

"No time to lose," I reminded him.

"Yes. I know, but—phew! Steady on, I shall explode!"

His portly form was designed more for comfort than speed, and passers-by turned to stare as the wheezing athlete chugged past, his face purple with exertion, and his socks hanging concertina-fashion about his ankles.

"Run on!" I encouraged him from the comfort of a well-sprung saddle. "Only another quarter of a mile to go."

All the same I *did* ease the pace slightly, because by then we'd reached the hill leading up to the Tech's main entrance.

The bell for afternoon school was sounding as we parked the machine in the school bicycle shed and rushed into the building, hot-foot for the carpenter's shop. . . . But we didn't get that far. As we hurried along the first corridor, a bespectacled character in a blue suit flickered into focus at the top of a staircase on our left.

"Oh golly, it's the Head!" croaked Bubblegum.

We skidded to a halt, and stood close together to hide the tell-tale chain.

"Why are you boys still in the corridor? Hurry up into your classroom," quoth the H.M.

"Yes, sir," said Bubblegum.

Term had only just started at the Tech, so I suppose the Head mistook me for one of the dozens of new boys who had just been added to their ranks. At any rate, he didn't ask who I was. Instead, he stood watching as we made tracks for a classroom further along the passage.

When we reached the door, Tucker whispered: "We'll have to go in, Milligan. He's still got us in his gunsights."

Now, this was rather a change from the programme as advertised; but I couldn't say anything with the Archbeak keeping tabs on us only a few yards away. Together we wheeled left through the door.

There was no master in the room, but sitting at a

front row desk was Spikey Andrews. He nearly had a heart attack when he saw me.

"What are you doing here, Milligan?" he gasped.

I pointed to the chain on my wrist.

"It's all the fault of this gruesome Bubblegum specimen," I explained. "He's gone and bished up the issue properly."

Spikey rocked with silent laughter.

"That's what I call a really smashing victory," he crowed. "We've not only got the Grammar School's flag; we've got a stranglehold on one of their personnel, too."

"Not for long," I assured him. "As soon as I can . . ."

"Look out; Old Snorker's coming!" hissed a pink-faced youth, sitting by the door.

Bubblegum leapt like a mountain goat, and fairly propelled me to a double desk in the back row.

And only just in time! As we reached our seats a heavy footfall sounded in the doorway, and the curiously-named O. Snorker, Esq., strode in to begin the lesson.

He was a stockily-built man, with shaggy eyebrows and receding hair. What his real name was I didn't know at the time, but "Snorker" seemed to fit him well enough. He crossed to the master's desk with only a casual glance at the thirty or so boys seated before him, and so failed to notice the strange face in their midst.

But no sooner had he sat down, than he sniffed the air like a well-trained bloodhound, and said: "It's stuffy in here. That wretched air-conditioning plant is overheating again. Open the window, Tucker!"

With a gulp of despair Bubblegum rose to his feet . . .

So did I! After all, I couldn't help myself; and together we sidled out of the desk and shuffled to the window, keeping our manacled hands out of sight. Then we each extended our free arm and pulled the window down.

Snorker stared at us in some bewilderment.

"It doesn't take two boys to open one window," he began. And then, as we performed a complicated about-turn to get back to our desks, he gave me a searching look.

"I don't seem to remember seeing you about the place before. What's your name?" he asked.

"Milligan, sir."

"You're new here, aren't you?"

"Oh yes, sir. I've never been here before," I replied truthfully.

Old Snorker continued to look puzzled as he thumbed his way through the register, wondering how he had come to overlook me. Finally he said: "Well, you don't belong in this class. You'd better go along to the headmaster's office, and find out which form you're supposed to be in."

Bubblegum cast a despairing glance at me, realizing that the game would be up as soon as I tried to move away. The situation called for some quick thinking.

"Please, sir, I don't know the way to the headmaster's office. Could Tucker come along and show me?" I asked.

Old Snorker nodded a grudging assent, whereupon we walked sedately to the door, trying not to look more like a pair of Siamese Twins than we could help.

This time we reached the carpenter's shop without further setback, and in two bats of an eyelid I'd grabbed a pair of pliers and a file and cut my way through the chain.

Tucker heaved a sigh of relief.

"Phew! Thank goodness! You won't find *me* taking any more prisoners in a hurry." He gave me a toothy smile and made tracks for his classroom, leaving me to make my escape from the building as best I could.

I hadn't much idea of the geography of the place, so I followed a corridor which looked as though it might lead in the required direction. But it didn't: and after five minutes of futile wandering I found myself passing Bubblegum's classroom once more. As I drew level, the door opened and our old friend O. Snorker came trundling out into the passage.

He gave me an old-fashioned look. "What are you doing here? I thought Tucker had taken you to the headmaster," he said.

"Yes, sir. Unfortunately, I er—got lost in transit, if you follow me, sir."

Old Snorker beetled at me from under his eyebrows, obviously wondering why half-witted characters like *me* should be inflicted on long-suffering schoolmasters like *him*. Then he said: "Follow me, boy: I'll take you along myself."

He set off along the corridor at a sprightly pace, while I trailed along behind racking my so-called brain in an effort to work out my next move.

In a matter of minutes I should be called upon to account for my presence within the precincts; and it was this gruesome predicament that caused a worried frown to cloud the features of yours truly, R. Milligan. You see, if once the facts became known, the headmaster of the Tech would almost certainly take off for a roof-level attack on Spikey and his brave warriors.

That would have been bad enough; but it would be

nothing to the purge that our headmaster at Sheldrake's would organize, if the two H.M.s got together and compared notes.

As a general rule, I have nothing but praise for Mr. Hunter, our headmaster (known out of earshot as the Head-hunter). Where discipline is concerned he believes in keeping us on a tight rein; but he's never unfair, and neither does he go beserk without good cause.

The only point on which he and Form 4 do not see eye to eye is this question of rivalry with the Technical School. He thinks we should remain dignified and aloof, and nothing rouses his wrath more quickly than the news that we've been ragging in public. So you see, there was every good reason why the news of the battle should not be allowed to come to his ears, when term started at the Grammar School next morning. Something would have to be done, I decided. A state of emergency had arisen!

Just then we reached the office. Old Snorker tapped on the door and walked in, leaving me in the corridor outside.

I wasted no time—I turned and pelted along the corridor as fast as I could run.

From behind me I heard a sudden commotion at the door of the headmaster's room; and the next second two bewildered schoolmasters were prancing about on the threshold, shouting orders.

"Stop! Hey, you there, whatever your name is, come back at once!" Thus spake Old Snorker.

"Wait, boy, wait. I want a word with you," called another voice, which I took to be the headmaster's.

As I gathered speed, I could hear the pursuit party getting into gear and calling for reinforcements to assist in the round-up. All along the passage, doors opened as puzzled form-masters popped their heads out to see what was causing the hoo-hah.

I didn't stop to explain. As the uninvited cuckoo in the nest, my one idea was to take wing and migrate to a safer clime as quickly as possible.

At the end of the passage I turned left, ran across a hall and out through an open door which led on to the quad. The school gates were ahead of me, but even as I made towards them there came a sound of tumult away to my right: and there was Old Snorker followed by a host of supporting troops rushing out on to the quad from another door, to cut off my line of escape.

A few yards away on my left was the bicycle shed, so I swerved in through the open door and went to ground in the farthest corner.

Had they spotted me? . . . I couldn't tell. All I could do was to crouch down on my knees, hardly daring to breathe, while the hurrying footsteps drew nearer and nearer towards my hiding place.

For the first time that afternoon luck was on my side. The footsteps on the quad came to an uncertain halt a few yards short of the shed door, while the pursuit party took time off to consider its next move.

"He can't have come this way, or we should have seen him. He must have run out through the front gate before we arrived," I heard Snorker say. "Either that, or he's still inside the building somewhere."

"But who is he?" demanded another member of the round-up party, who wasn't abreast of the latest developments.

"We don't really know. Some new boy who appears to be frightened of coming to school," Snorker replied. "A nervous type, obviously. He told me his name, but

I can't remember what it was. I'll go back to the office and see if I can trace him in the register."

Then the footsteps died away and I was able to abandon my attempt to break the European breath-holding record. As I scrambled to my feet I noticed that what I had been kneeling on was a screwed-up bundle of towelling in a delicate shade of off-white—or perhaps pale black would describe the colour better. I shook it out. . . . just as I'd thought, it was the Sheldrake banner, jettisoned by Spikey when he had parked his bike before afternoon school.

My first idea was to smuggle the flag out of the enemy's stronghold without more ado; but on second thoughts I decided to let Spikey do the job for me. There was always a chance that I might run into more trouble before I was clear of the premises. If that should happen the tell-tale evidence might be discovered, and then the whole story was bound to leak out.

With this in mind I folded the banner into a neat roll and pushed it well down to the bottom of Spikey's spacious saddle-bag. The odds were that he wouldn't look inside before setting off on his homeward journey, by which time Jigger and I would be lying in wait, ready to claim our property.

So far so good. Now I was all set to make my escape. I made a furtive reconnaissance through the crack of the door, and found that the coast wasn't as clear as I'd thought! A master had been posted outside in the quad where he could keep tabs on the school gates, in case I was still on the premises. This *wasn't* so good! I didn't want to spend the last afternoon of the holidays bottled up in a shed inside the enemy camp.

I glanced round my hideout. *Bottled up* was a fair

description, because in addition to the rows of bicycles there were half a dozen wire crates filled with empty school milk bottle waiting to be collected. The faint glimmerings of an idea glowed in the Milligan brain.

The master on sentry-go would be looking for a wandering scholar: furthermore, he didn't know me by sight. All right, then; if I could act the part of a smart lad assisting with the milk round, there was a chance that I could get past him without suspicion.

It was worth trying. I grabbed a couple of the wire crates and marched boldly out of the shed, clanking the bottles and whistling the latest hit tune at full pressure.

The master glanced at me with passing interest. I wished him good afternoon and trundled on with my rattling cargo, while he stood by and watched me, quite unaware that I was the nervous truant he was supposed to be looking out for.

I reached the gate in safety. The time had come, I decided, to call an unofficial strike in the milk-round business, so I plonked down my bottles by the gate-post, and hurried away down the road with never a backward glance.

Jigger Johnson was waiting for me on the corner. "What's been going on?" he wanted to know.

"Oh, nothing much. Just a minor hoo-hah about a so-called new boy who wouldn't stay put." And I told him how I had been pursued by O. Snorker and his posse.

"Pity you didin't keep your eyes open for our flag while you were prowling round the precincts," Jigger said.

"I did! And what's more it's in the bag—Spike's

saddle-bag to be precise," I answered. "I think this calls for *Operation Ambush*, don't you?"

At four o'clock we took up action stations outside the Technical School gates; and at five minutes past the hour we closed in on Spikey Andrews as he wheeled his bike on to the road.

"A word with you, Spikey," I greeted him. "We'd like our banner back, if you don't mind."

Spikey grinned. "I'm afraid you're going to be unlucky—it's missing. It was in the bike shed before school, and now it's gone!"

"I wouldn't be too sure about that," I said: and before he could stop me I'd whipped back the flap of his saddle-bag and retrieved our dog-eared property.

Spike's grin faded and he opened his eyes in surprise. "Gosh! How did that get there?"

He made a movement to snatch the flag from me, but I backed away out of range. For a moment I thought he was going to drop his bike and come rushing into the attack. Then he changed his mind: after all, he was outnumbered two to one.

"Thanks for looking after it for us," I said. "Of course, you realize that you can't claim a victory for this afternoon's battle now that you haven't got the flag to prove it!"

Spikey glowered at us for some seconds in sullen silence. Then he said: "All right. We'll call it quits—this time But I'm warning you Sheldrake specimens, you'd better watch your step. We'll get our own back for this, you see!"

And there was something in his tone which suggested that this was no idle threat.

PRIVATE ENTERPRISE

NEXT morning, term started at the Grammar School; and it started with a bit of a shock.

Alfie Cutforth was first with the news, as usual; and even before I'd had time to remove my cycling clips he came bounding up to the door of the bicycle shed, twittering his woeful tidings.

"I say! What do you think, Milligan? We've got to have morning assembly in the library in future," he announced. "We can't use the Great Hall any more. It's got beetle!"

"That's nothing new," I told him. "I've often spotted an odd cockroach popping out of the woodwork to hear what the Head was woffling about during assembly. They enjoy a spot of dry rot, you know."

"I don't mean ordinary black beetles—this is something a jolly sight more serious!" Alfie went on. "According to what I overheard Mr. Birkinshaw saying to Mr. Frisby, there's a plague of death-watch beetles eating their way through the beams in the roof. And what's more the Hall's been put out of bounds, so that proves it."

He turned and stared in fascinated horror at the Great Hall across the quad. I think he was hoping to see the ancient roof come crashing down at any moment, as the champing jaws of the villainous insects delivered their last death-dealing bite.

In this, he was unlucky. The time-weathered building stood gaunt and massive as it had done for the last two hundred years, and no amount of wishful thinking on the part of A. Cutforth could shake so much as a tile off the roof.

The bell for assembly sounded. Alfie came out of his trance, and together we made our way indoors for the start of another term.

Now, I'd written off Cutforth's news-bulletin as another of his well-known attempts to spread alarm and despondency. But it turned out that for once in his life he had hit the nail on the head—or very nearly!

Morning assembly was held in the library; and after the Head-hunter had cheered us up by saying we'd all got to work till our brains sizzled, he passed on to the usual beginning-of-term announcements.

"I have received a report from the architect who examined the Great Hall during the holidays," he began. "As you know, the building is the oldest part of the school, and dates back to the days of the Founder. Unfortunately, the ravages of time have left their mark and the examination has shown that a great deal must be done to the structure of the Hall before it can again be rendered safe and serviceable."

He prattled on for ten minutes about the history of the Great Hall and all it stood for, and held forth at some length upon the traditions of the school and the ideas of the Founder, Sir William Sheldrake (1669–1745).

I won't weary you with the entire oration, because the Head-hunter is apt to be a trifle long-winded on the subject of scholastic gobbledeygook. The nub of his argument was that the Hall was in poor shape; the roof, in particular, was in a very bad way, thanks to woodworm and sundry termites using ye olde oaken beams for their pestilential picnics. Unless something was done, quoth the Head-hunter, the Hall which had been standing for so long in its own grounds would shortly be sitting down in them. (I give you the gist: the H.M. phrased it somewhat differently.)

The Education Authorities were sympathetic. They were willing to repair the damage with steel girders and cement, so that the Hall's foundations would no longer quiver at the sound of six hundred boys singing the school song. But they were *not* prepared to go to the further expense of making good the building in its former style of architecture.

You couldn't blame them for this, really. After all, you need to be careful about spending money provided by hard-working ratepayers; and the feeling at Educational H.Q. was that if we wanted to restore the roof as per Sir W. Sheldrake's original blue-print, it was up to us to find the balance af the money.

Now, we're proud of our school's history. It dates back to the days before anyone had ever invented County Education Committees; and the prospect of having our Hall patched up to look like a flat-roofed, pre-fabricated jam factory was enough to make the worthy Sir W. rotate in his tomb—to say nothing of the *tut-tutting* it would cause amongst the governors, staff, Old-Sheldrakians and boys.

Very well then, demanded the Head-hunter (and again I précis his well-chosen words). Very well then; were we, as a school, prepared to raise the rest of the money needed to replace ye oaken beams, and restore ye gabled roof, so that the old shack still looked as it was wont to do in the days of yore?

We didn't shout out the answer, because you don't interrupt headmasters when they are making speeches, but by this time the whole school was solid in its support for the H.M.'s suggestion. . . . Of *course* we'd raise the money! . . . Leave it to us! . . . We'd show 'em! . . . Good old Sheldrake's! . . . Up the Grammar! . . .

There'd be no corrugated iron and wallboard about *our* seat of learning, if we had anything to do with it!

We discussed the matter amongst ourselves during morning break. Everyone seemed in favour of pressing forward with some money-making scheme—everyone, that is, except Alfie Cutforth who went pale with panic at the thought of having to stump up a contribution out of his own pocket.

"This business isn't going to be too easy," Jigger observed thoughtfully, as he champed his way through a rubbery school bun. "According to what the Head said, I gather we shall need at least another £6,000 on top of the grant which the County Education people are going to fork out."

"The whole thing's crazy, if you ask me," grumbled Alfie. "Spending all that money on fancy rafters and stuff. Besides, we should never be able to scrape up that amount, anyway."

"Of course we would!" countered a dozen optimists in the same breath.

"How?" jibed Alfie. "Just you tell me where it's going to come from—just tell me, that's all!"

"I've got an unused three p stamp you can have for a kick-off," remarked Boko generously. "And then, if we could persuade some scrap-iron merchant to give us twenty-five pence for Cutforth's two-wheeled fire-escape, we'd be well away."

Alfie doesn't like jokes about his bicycle. He doesn't like Boko, either.

"You shut up and mind your own business, Phipps," he retorted in the high-pitched squawk he always uses when he's in a bate. "Nobody asked you to butt in. My bike's as good as yours any day, so shut up about it, unless you want to cop a packet."

Boko favoured him with a sad sweet smile, and

said: "What I like about you, Cutforth, is your friendly manner, and your keenness to help the school. . . . But the thing I like *best* about you is your bicycle. It never loses its temper when somebody makes a joke."

The gentle sarcasm was wasted on Cutforth. He snorted, and swung the conversation back to the topic under discussion.

"If you ask me, I'd say the Head-hunter must be stark raving haywire if he imagines he's going to get all that rhino out of us," he said ungraciously. "Why, it works out at about ten pounds a head for each chap in the school."

"You needn't worry, anyway, Alfie. No one will be asked to part with their pocket-money," I consoled him. "If you'd kept your ears open in assembly this morning, you'd know that the idea is for each form to get together and earn what they can. Take Form 4, for instance. Thirty chaps ought to be able to rake in . . ."

I paused to consider a flaw in the optimism which had just occurred to me. It was all very well to talk airily of thirty chaps raising an average of—say—a pound a head, but when we got down to brass tacks I knew there'd be such keen competition to earn an honest shekel that there wouldn't be enough odd-jobbery to go round.

"Go on, Milligan. You were telling us how simple it's going to be," prompted Alfie. He poked his head forward and put on a knowing smirk. "If you ask me, you won't get thirty pence out of our Form, let alone thirty pounds—you mark my words!"

I wasn't going to stand for that sort of nonsense from A. Cutforth.

"Don't you believe it," I said. "Why, Jigger and

Boko and me, and one or two more, could earn that little lot, easily."

"Bet you a million pounds you couldn't!"

"Have you got a million pounds?"

"Well, no. But I bet you a choc-ice, then!"

If I'd known what a hoo-hah I was letting myself in for I might have thought twice before accepting a challenge so bristling with snags. On the other hand, I couldn't climb down now, or Alfie would have laughed himself into a coma at my expense. Besides, if the Hall was to be saved, it was up to someone to start the ball rolling.

"You can keep your choc-ices," I told him. "And you can quote me as saying that Form 4's contribution towards raising the new roof is as good as in the bag already!"

A rash prophecy, if ever I made one! But the fatal words had been uttered before witnesses. There could be no going back now, without leaving a fair-sized blot on Form 4's stainless reputation.

As soon as I had finished my prep that evening, I pedalled round to Jigger's house to discuss ways and means of floating some water-tight wheeze that would bring the money rolling in.

I met Boko on the way, so I took him along with me: and then the three of us put our heads together and got down to business in the tool shed.

For the first half hour the discussion wandered round in circles getting nowhere. We had plenty of ideas, some of which dazzled us by their brilliance when first suggested . . . and then petered out like damp squibs when we saw how impossible they would be to carry out.

"We're getting out of our depth, that's the trouble," Jigger decided at length. "It's crazy to go on woffling about gymkhanas and yacht races and flower shows. I vote we try and find people who want their gardens dug, or their windows cleaned, or something like that."

Boko wasn't impressed. "We shall be suffering from window-cleaners' elbow by the time we've done £30 worth of pane-polishing," he objected. "Besides, it would take about a hundred years to find enough people who wanted that amount of work done."

"Well, you suggest something better then," Jigger retorted warmly. "All very well for you to sit there like a spare dinner pouring cold water on other people's brain-waves, while they do all the donkey work! I'd like to see you—"

"All right, all *right*! I'm not trying to pour cold water on any donkey's dinner," replied Boko, mixing the metaphors more thoroughly. "All I said was——"

"Oh, shut up arguing, both of you!" I broke in. "Jigger's scheme is all right for a start, but it's not enough by itself. What we want is something like a—well, er . . ." I searched my brain frantically for an idea. "Well, how would it be if we were to organize something like, say, for instance, a jumble sale?"

"Jumble sale!" snorted Boko, raising despairing eyes to the ceiling. "Of all the feeble, futile, fatuous ideas I ever heard, I reckon a jumble sale takes the certificate of merit for weak-kneed, antiseptic eye-wash! You'll be organizing knitting parties and needle-work rallies next, I shouldn't wonder!"

Coming from Boko this was high praise indeed. The lad often says one thing when he means just the opposite; and I knew, then, that he thought a jumble sale would be a jolly good idea, and was kicking himself for not having suggested it first.

"Your turn now," I told him. "We're all waiting

with our ears out on strings to hear of some brilliant project from the *A*-level brain of B. Phipps!"

Boko scratched his nose thoughtfully for a few moments. Then, suddenly, he jumped to his feet, his eyes gleaming with inspiration.

"I've got it!" he cried, smiting himself on the forehead as proof that his mind was working at more than the usual horse-power. "I've got it! Cycle speedway racing! We'll build a track on the old bombed site, fix up some race meetings, and then go round with the hat!"

Jigger and I goggled at him in wide-eyed admiration. Cycle speedway racing! Why hadn't we thought of it before? Once we had something like that properly organized, we would have nothing to do but sit back and watch the money rolling in. And the old bombed site would be just the place.

Judging by the number of open spaces dotted about, which used to be shops and houses, I reckon our suburb had its fair share of trouble during the war. Some of the bombed sites have been made into car parks, and on others there are new buildings; but there is still one unhappily-looking ruin just off the main shopping centre, and it was this that Boko had in mind.

"We may have to tidy it up a bit before we can use it as a race track," he explained. "Still, it shouldn't be difficult. We've only got to let the chaps in our form know what we're doing and we'll get no end of characters falling over themselves to help with the good work."

Boko was delighted with his little plan. He breathed on his fingernails and polished them on the lapel of his jacket to indicate that bright ideas came easily to the brain of B. Phipps.

"We could challenge the Tech to a programme of

cycle races instead of mock battles," Jigger suggested with mounting enthusiasm. "If each side brings along all the spectators they can lay hands on, and they each make a contribution to the funds, we ought to get —well, quite a lot, anyway."

We were all feeling pleased with ourselves by this time. The more we considered Boko's idea, the better we liked in. A smart lad, this Phipps! We had misjudged him. Beneath his hairy cranium throbbed a super-charged brain unit capable of exporting watertight wheezes at short notice. . . . Hearty cheers for Boko!

We now had three money-making activities, so we appointed Jigger as Hon. Treasurer. Before the meeting broke up, he made the following entry in his diary——

GREAT HALL ROOF REPAIR FUND
(1) Odd Jobbery . . .
(2) Cycle Speedway Racing. . . .
(3) Jumble Sale . . .

And against each item he left a space for recording the profits of the enterprise. All very efficient and business-like, we thought. It would not be long before things started moving in a big way.

How right we were! . . . But what a pity they didn't move in the way we were expecting!

SPIKEY BAITS THE TRAP

Two days later the odd-jobbery department obtained its first order; and curiously enough it was our old enemy, Spikey Andrews, who presented us with what seemed like a good business proposition.

Jigger had met him the previous day on his way home from school, and had thrown out a challenge for a series of bicycle races on the bombed site, to take place at some future date when the track had been prepared.

I think Jigger must have mentioned the worthy cause underlying our scheme, because Spikey seemed to know all about it when he called round at my house the following evening.

I was rather surprised to see him. The leader of the Tech Brigade is not what you might call a frequent visitor at the Milligan homestead.

"Hullo!" he greeted me with a grin, when I opened the door. "I've heard you Grammar specimens are on the lookout for odd jobs and stuff."

I admitted the fact.

"Well, I can put you on to something right away. One of the masters at our school is moving house next week, and he wants someone to clean the place up before he goes in. I told him I knew some chaps who'd be glad of the job, and he gave me the go-head signal to fix up the details. You should make at least a pound for your funds, because there's quite a lot that needs doing."

Spikey's manner was friendly—more friendly than I

should have thought possible; but I put that down to the fact that he recognized a worthy cause when he saw one, and wanted to rally round and help. So when he gave me the particulars I thanked him, and clinched the deal then and there.

No. 71, Elm Gardens, was the address of the so-called desirable residence—a red brick, semi-detached villa in a row of similar houses. It had been empty for some weeks and the general idea was that I should chivvy a handful of eager helpers along to the house on the following Saturday and give the place a good wash-and-brush-up.

"I expect Mr. Howard—that's the name of our master—I expect he'll breeze along round about tea-time, and settle up with you. I'll tell him to do that, anyway," Spikey said.

"Thanks very much. It's jolly decent of you to go to all this trouble."

"Oh, that's all right. I shall enjoy seeing how you get on," he said. And once again came the friendly grin—almost *too* friendly, I thought.

Anyway, the three founder-members of the Sheldrake working party, armed to the teeth with mops, buckets and dustpans, reported for duty the following Saturday morning. We took J. O. Stagg along with us as well: the dear boy rather fancies himself as an expert on household gadgets, and he was straining at the leash to try out an old vacuum cleaner that he had salvaged from some scrap heap.

As we turned in at the gate of No. 71, Alfie Cutforth approached from the other end of the road, clasping a bulky bundle wrapped in sacking.

"I say, Milligan. Would you mind if I joined in and helped?" he asked, as he came up.

"What—*you*! But dash it all, Cutforth, you did

your best to pour cold water on the idea. You said we'd never manage it."

"Well, yes, I know," he agreed, somewhat sheepishly. "But seeing that you're really going ahead with it, I thought I'd like to do my whack, too."

I couldn't very well refuse him, now that he was a reformed character who had seen the error of his ways. "All right, then," I agreed. "But what have you brought in that sack?"

"A rather decent set of chimney-sweeping brushes," he said brightly. "My dad bought them second-hand, but he's never used them.'

"But *you* can't sweep chimneys. That's a skilled occupation."

"Maybe it is, but it won't do any harm if I just have a bash at cleaning the flues in the boiler, or something. Of course, if you don't want my help. . . ."

"Come on in, and get on with it, then," said Jigger, impatient to get to grips with the job on hand.

I had forgotten to ask Spikey for the key, and as both the outside doors were locked, Jigger had to climb in *via* the kitchen window and open the front door for us. But this didn't delay us for long, and within a matter of minutes the working party was in its shirt sleeves raring for action.

Jigger filled his bucket from the cold tap and started scouring the floorboards, room by room, while I skipped round in front of him raising a major dust storm with a yard brush. Alfie wrote his name in the grime coating the kitchen walls, and then spent half an hour joining up the rods of his sweeping brushes.

Boko couldn't quite think what to do. He wandered round vaguely for a time, and then set to work oiling the locks with a tin of mowing-machine oil which he found in the coal-hole.

I think we should have got on more quickly without Stagg. His dilapidated vacuum cleaner began shedding odd parts as soon as we set foot in the house, and it took some time to gather them all together and pile them back inside the machine. But at last he was ready:

"You needn't bother sweeping any more, Milligan. This will do the job in half the time," he announced in his rich, plummy voice which always makes him sound as though he's talking in capital letters. He favoured me with a bright, shining smile and plugged in his lead to an electric point. Then he switched on.

There came a grinding, whirring noise from the depths of the cleaner. Then a blinding blue flash, followed by tongues of flame spurting from the machine and leaping towards the ceiling. A moment later the flapping dust-bag was flaming merrily, and the smell of burning rubber pervaded the room.

Well, that knocked the shine off Staggers' smile all right. He rushed to the switch, tripped over the trailing flex and fell headlong, just as Jigger swooshed the contents of his cleaning bucket over the dust-bag. . . . Or, to be precise, he would have dowsed the dust-bag, if the Staggers hadn't crash-landed on the target area, and stopped the whole pailful with the back of his neck.

"Ow! Gosh! Mind out, you clumsy bazooka!" he gasped, struggling to his feet with water cascading down his pullover, and splashing round his ankles.

The vacuum cleaner was still sparking and crackling like a firework display, so I pulled the switch out of the socket, grabbed the machine in one of its cooler spots, and belted out into the garden, leaving behind me a vapour trail that would have done credit to a jet fighter.

As I heaved the flaming contraption on to the nearest flower-bed, I was aware that my actions were being followed by an interested crowd of spectators.

I glanced towards the road. . . . Hanging over the garden gate was Spikey Andrews, accompanied by a sizeable gaggle of cronies from the Tech.

"We thought we'd just pop along to see if you were getting on all right," Spikey said, switching on his broadest grin.

I thanked him politely.

"You've made a good start, I see," smirked Bubble-gum Tucker, pointing to the smouldering remains on the flower-bed. "I thought the idea was to clean the place up—not burn it down!"

At that moment the bedraggled Staggers came squelching down the garden path, heading for home and dry clothing. The crowd round the gate went into hysterics.

"Old Father Neptune in person!" chanted Spikey. "Gosh, I am glad we came. I wouldn't have missed this for anything!"

It was on the tip of my tongue to tell him to go and take a running jump at himself, but I remembered in time that it was all due to Spikey and Co. that we had been given the job in the first place. A tactful retort seemed to be called for, so I said: "You don't *have* to stay and watch if you don't want to. We can manage quite well by ourselves, you know."

"That's all right," said Spikey, perching himself comfortably on the gatepost as though settling down for a long spell. "We're in no hurry. Just carry on and don't mind us!"

I went back into the house muttering darkly.

"Spikey's gruesome specimens are outside laughing

themselves silly at our expense," I told Jigger. "Let's take good care that nothing else goes wrong."

Perhaps I should have said that, because if ever there was a day when nothing went right, that day was this day, if you follow me.

We hadn't been working for more than five minutes before thumps and cries for assistance sounded from upstairs. I trundled aloft to investigate, and found that the SOS calls came from Boko, who had brilliantly locked himself into the front bedroom.

"I can't get out!" he explained through the jamb of the door. "I was testing the lock after oiling it and the key snapped off short when I turned it!"

I couldn't do anything from my side of the door because the keyhole was wedged solid with the end of the broken key.

"You'll have to get out through the window," I decided.

"Yes, but how? You don't expect me to make a parachute out of my handkerchief and bale out over the coal-bunker, do you?"

The liberation of B. Phipps wasted nearly half the morning. First of all I had to make a house-to-house tour of the neighbourhood trying to borrow a ladder; and when at last I staggered back to No. 71 bearing a chronic contraption with rickety rungs, I found that it wouldn't quite reach the first-floor window.

The Technical spectators went wild with delight. They whistled and cheered as Boko climbed over the sill and hung in space trying to touch down on the top of the ladder.

"Golly, this is better than television," approved Bubblegum. "Decent of them to lay on a free show just for us, isn't it?"

At the second attempt I managed to guide Boko's

swinging ankles on to the head of the ladder. We descended amidst a salvo of applause and requests for autographs from the mob milling round the gate.

"Take this prehistoric ruin back to No. 59—and mind the rungs don't drop off," I told Boko. "Then go and find a carpenter or someone to fix that lock, and tell him to bring a proper ladder."

Jigger appeared at the front door at that moment. "He'd better get a chimney sweep, too, while he's about it," he said grimly. "Alfie's gone and bished up the issue properly in the dining-room."

"Oh, fish-hooks!" I groaned, and tottered inside to inspect the damage.

It wasn't until Jigger had finished spring-cleaning the dining-room that Cutforth felt the urge to sweep the chimney. Glowing with enthusiasm, he had pushed up the brush and unleashed a landslide of soot all over the newly-scrubbed floor. You never saw such a devastated area as that room; window-sills, picture rails and cupboards were plastered with a thick black deposit, while a dense fog of soot swirled about, blotting out nine-tenths of the visibility.

"You beetle-headed clodpoll!" I stormed at the black-faced Cutforth. "What on earth did you want to go and stir up all this hoo-hah for?"

A gleam of white teeth flashed from the nigger minstrel by the fireplace as Alfie squawked back: "Well, how was I to know it was going to happen? I'd like to see you do better!"

I hurried across the room and tugged at the rod protruding from the fireplace. Down came another hundredweight of soot, but the brush remained firm. Then Jigger and Alfie joined me in a tug-o'-war, and together we heaved-ho like a trio of Volga boatmen. . . . But all to no purpose.

We were still tugging twenty minutes later when Boko returned with a chimney sweep and a carpenter, whom he had been lucky enough to find just as they were knocking off work for the week-end.

The sweep was a cheerful customer. He laughed himself almost white in the face when he saw the state we were in.

"Proper lot of Charleys, you are," he chirruped goodhumouredly. "That's what comes of pulling against the bristles. Once you start pushing the brush up, you don't want it to come down again till you've cleared the chimney-pot. Might as well try to open an umbrella in a drain-pipe."

He set to work to free the tightly-wedged bristles. This was no easy job, even for the expert; and when at last he succeeded, he charged us twenty pence for services rendered, and departed still chortling and gurgling like a bathroom waste-pipe.

Yells of derisive mirth wafting through the window told us that he'd paused at the garden gate to tell Spikey and Co. how the working party had put its foot in things, right up to the knee-joint.

Shortly afterwards the carpenter shouldered his ladder and stonked off, leaving us thirty pence the poorer. As it happened, we couldn't raise enough ready cash to meet his demands, and Boko had to promise to go round to the builders and settle up on the following Monday morning.

"This is chronic," groaned Jigger. "That's fifty pence down the drain, and we came here to *make* money, not to spend it."

"Perhaps we could charge it up to this Mr. Howard chap," suggested Alfie hopefully.

"Of course we can't. He didn't ask us to provide new keys—or to plaster the place with soot, either."

"No good moaning about it, anyway," I decided. "Let's get the place looking clean and tidy, and then if he's in a generous mood he may, perhaps, give us enough to clear the expenses and leave a bit over for the fund."

"*If . . . perhaps . . .* he *may . . .*" echoed Boko, picking on the words that really mattered.

Anyway, we called a lunch break at that juncture and trooped home to refuel on sausages and mash. An hour later we paraded for the afternoon shift; and this time Stagg J. O. was back with the team, his garments dehydrated and his feet dry-shod.

Things went with more of a swing after the lunch break. For one thing, Spikey Andrews and his satellites had grown weary of mocking our capers and had taken themselves off. This meant that we could settle down to work with carefree minds; and though I say it myself, we really put our backs into it that afternoon, scouring, scraping and cleaning like nobody's business.

We polished the bathroom taps as though they were the Crown Jewels: we black-leaded the boiler and burnished the boot-scraper as though they were priceless family heirlooms.

In a couple of hours the place was so clean you could have eaten your dinner off the kitchen floor. I'm not saying you would have *enjoyed* your dinner under those conditions, because it would have tasted of carbolic soap; but all the same, no one could deny that we'd made a very workmanlike job of No. 71 Elm Gardens, London, N.W.

At four o'clock Jigger wrung out his mop for the last time and said: "Well, that's that! There's nothing else to do now, unless we start dusting the nutty slack in the coalhole."

"Thank goodness," breathed Boko. "I've been massaging the scullery floorboards for so long I can feel housemaid's knee coming on. I vote we call it a day and go home."

"We can't all go," I pointed out. "One of us has got to stay to receive the grateful owner's contribution to our funds."

"Bags not me, then. I want my tea," grunted Alfie, gathering up his chimney rods.

"I'm feeling a bit peckish, too," Jigger admitted.

"And it's high time I was getting along," said the Staggers importantly. "I'm working on the blue-print for a new secret weapon I'm inventing to use against the Tech, and it's just reached rather a tricky stage of development."

So in the end I volunteered to stay by myself, while my fellow workers shouldered their mops and marched off, well satisfied with the afternoon's work.

I hadn't been waiting long when I heard the click of the garden gate. I hurried to the front door, all beams and smiles, to welcome the happy householder.

But it wasn't Mr. Howard. It was a motherly-looking woman with a bulging shopping-bag. She looked a little puzzled when she saw me standing there.

"I didn't think there'd be anyone in before half-past four," she began. "At least, that's the time Mr. Howard said he'd be along to tell me what cleaning he wanted done."

This time it was my turn to look puzzled.

"But the cleaning has been done already," I explained. "A whole gang of us have been hard at it all day. Come inside and see for yourself!"

She gave me an old-fashioned look and followed me into the house.

"I don't understand this at all," she said, goggling in bewilderment through the door of the spotless dining-room. "Mr. Howard said quite definitely as how there'd be three hours' scrubbing for me this evening."

"There must be some mistake. He told *us* to do it," I pointed out. "Not personally, of course, because I've never met him. We got the message from one of the boys at his school."

"Well, I *do* know him personally, seeing as my eldest is in his form, and what's more I got *my* instructions from Mr. Howard himself. 'Mrs. Tucker,' he says when he called round at my house last Wednesday, 'Mrs. Tucker, I've got a little job you might care to help me out with,' he says . . ."

The room swam before my eyes and I gaped at her in dismay. *Mrs. Tucker!* The mother of the gruesome Bubblegum T. . . . In a flash the whole hideous plot became crystal clear.

Spikey Andrews must have heard from Bubblegum that Mrs. Tucker had agreed to conduct the mopping-up operations: he knew, too, that we were on the look-out for a similar engagement. Here, then, was a way to make the Grammar School working party look extremely foolish, and waste a whole day in unpaid labour. No wonder the Tech had been feeling so pleased with themselves all morning!

I could have kicked myself for not spotting the crafty subterfuge at the start. Now it was too late to do anything about it. I forced my mind back to Mrs. Tucker's observations.

". . . and it doesn't look as though there's much left for me to do," she was saying. "By rights, of course, you ought to have the money for the job . . ."

My heart leapt. Perhaps, after all, we had not laboured in vain!

". . . but as it happens Mr. Howard paid me in advance and I spent it all on a new pair of shoes for my Albert!"

I swallowed hard and took a grip on myself. The thought of the obnoxious Bubblegum waltzing round in a pair of new shoes earned by the sweat of our brows was too much for flesh and blood to stand.

"I'd better be going, then," I mumbled. "Mr. Howard won't want to pay for the job twice over."

"No. I don't suppose he will. Never mind, better luck next time," Mrs. Tucker consoled me.

At that moment the click of the garden gate sounded once more, and she glanced through the window into the front garden.

"Why, here's Mr. Howard coming now," she announced brightly. "Perhaps you'd like to have a word with him. I'll introduce you, if you like."

I followed the direction of her glance. Striding up the garden path was a figure I recognized only too well—it was the one-and-only Old Snorker, in person!

"Don't bother," I said hastily, making tracks for the back door. "Mr. Howard and I have already met. Somehow I don't think I shall be too popular if he finds me making myself at home in his dining-room."

I slipped through the kitchen door and waited till O. Snorker, Esq., had been admitted by the front entrance. Then I hurried past the dining-room windows with averted gaze. I reached the gate without incident, and as I was closing it behind me a cry of recognition rang out from the house.

"Hey, you there! You're the boy who escaped from my class. Come back! I want an explanation. . . ."

I slammed the gate behind me and hurried down the road. I had no wish to see Old Snorker again. Things were bad enough already: there was no point in making them worse with long-winded explanations that wouldn't help matters, anyway.

I rounded the corner and slowed to a walking pace. There was no sign of pursuit, so I reckoned I could afford to calm down and take things easily. But I *couldn't* calm down. My mind was seething with baffled fury. All that hard work for nothing! All that hoo-hah just to give Spikey a good laugh and Bubble-gum a pair of new shoes!

They'd caught us napping this time, right enough, but I meant to take jolly good care that it didn't happen again. Just let old Spikey try any more funny business at our expense, I said to myself. Just let him *try*, that's all!

TROUBLE ON THE TRACK

WE spent most of our free time during the next few days in working out plans for the cycle speedway.

On paper, this looked like being the best of our three money-making enterprises. All we should have to do, we told ourselves, would be to stage an afternoon's sport, pass the hat round amongst the dense throng of spectators, and then go home to tea staggering under the weight of the collection.

"There's nothing to it, really," Boko said during morning break on the Tuesday after our spring-cleaning fiasco. "It'll be a jolly sight easier than scrubbing floorboards—quite apart from the shortage of floorboards in need of a scrub."

There was some truth in this. By this time every

form in the school had organized working parties of one sort or another, and there just weren't enough jobs to go round. You couldn't turn a corner anywhere in the district without stumbling over Grammar School volunteers trimming hedges, mowing lawns or cleaning windows in aid of the Great Hall Fund. Some of the chaps had been lucky enough to get early morning newspaper rounds: others delivered groceries on Saturdays. But this steady employment wasn't easy to come by; and in the face of such cut-throat competition it seemed that the best way of earning our quota would be to launch out with Boko's bright idea, before anybody else thought of doing the same thing.

"Let's get down to brass tacks and decide where we're going to hold the races," said Jigger. "So far as I can see, there's only one site you could adapt as a speedway, and that's the one just off Victoria Crescent."

"Bright boy! That's the dump I had in mind," Boko answered. "I vote we go and have a look at it on our way home from school."

Before the war, so I'm told, Victoria Crescent had been a thoroughfare of old-fashioned houses, with flights of steps leading up to the front doors, and basements sunk below street level. Then had come the bomb which had flattened out most of the tall, thin houses and left only a fringe of derelict ruins round the edge of the target area.

At first glance things didn't look too promising when we went along that afternoon to cast an eye over our prospective speedway. We hadn't expected to find the place as flat as a billiard table; but we *had* hoped for something with rather less gradient than the foothills of the Himalayas.

Mind you, the site had been tidied up after a fashion.

The rubble had been shot into the basements of the old buildings; but there were still so many half-bricks and pieces of window-frame dotted about amongst the natural vegetation that the place seemed more suitable for obstacle races than for cycle sprints.

"Wow! We can't race on this. We shall all finish up with square wheels," prophesied Boko.

"Don't be such a gloomy specimen," Jigger reproved him. "By the time our famous working party has had a go at it, you'll need a spirit level to find where the bumps are."

This was an exaggeration: though if you had seen the place a week later, you'd have been forced to admit that there was some truth in Jigger's wild claim.

"What we'll do," Jigger went on, surveying the ruins with a critical eye, "is to round up a bevy of volunteers from our form and put them to work at once."

This we did. Offers of help came pouring in as soon as the news of our venture spread round the school, and for the next few evenings the bombed site was the scene of workmanlike activity.

Boko organized a gang to fill up the potholes. Clarke, Evans and Scuttersthorp, a trio of Form 4 worthies, cleared the jungle of undergrowth and overgrowth which had been sprouting unchecked for some years. Alfie Cutforth lumbered round with a wheelbarrow engaged on some mysterious task of his own. . . . And J. O. Stagg turned his talents to good purpose by inventing a type of bulldozer hitherto unknown to workers in the demolition trade.

It consisted of a sheet of corrugated iron suspended lengthways in front of his bicycle wheel, and attached to the front forks by a bracket. There were various pulleys, rollers and armchair castors sprinkled here and there amongst the mechanism, and according to the Staggers the whole apparatus was designed on strictly scientific principles.

"Between you and me, Milligan, I'm rather proud of this little gadget," he confided as he trundled his rattling contraption along to the demolition site after tea one evening. "It's a cross between a hand-operated bulldozer and a miniature snow-plough."

"Really!" I marvelled, aghast at the wonders of modern engineering.

"Oh, yes. I shall call it the Stagg-dozer if I decide to take out a patent for it. I haven't tried it out yet because I only got the idea during Mr. Birkinshaw's history lesson yesterday, but I'm pretty sure I'm on to a good thing this time."

"That'll be a change, anyway," I said. "And you're certain there's nothing to blow up, or catch fire, or drop to pieces?"

"Good heavens, no! It's guaranteed foolproof. Mind you, I may have to make one or two minor adjustments, but I'm not expecting any serious snags. You watch, and I'll give you a demonstration."

He wheeled the clanking mechanism on to the ruins and swung his leg over the saddle. . . .

The only disadvantage of the famous Stagg-dozer was that it didn't work. In theory, the idea was that as the bicycle moved forward the cow-catching device in the foreground would brush aside the obstructions in its path. In practice, however, the accumulation of rubbish brought the machine to a standstill in the first yard, and from then onwards the going was so heavy that Stagg might just as well have tried to pedal through the side of a cliff.

"Needs a slight adjustment," he gasped, red in the face with his exertions. "I probably didn't allow sufficient margin for metal fatigue when I made my calculations."

I tut-tutted in kindly sympathy. It's a waste of breath telling the lad that his unpractical brainwaves are nothing more than shatter-pated moonshine, because half his time he lives in a little world of his own, in which the only thing that matters is the latest invention of that top-ranking scientist, J. O. Stagg. And he's been playing this game of make-believe for so long now, he's almost persuaded himself that it's true.

So I wasn't worried by the failure of the Staggdozer. Even without its help the work of demolition and track-laying proceeded at a cracking pace. More than once, policemen paused to cock a suspicious eye at the turmoil and ask us what we thought we were playing at. But they strolled on again when we explained that we were beautifying the landscape in a good cause, and had no intention of indulging in any unlawful skullduggery.

By the middle of the following week the speedway was so well advanced that I sought out Spikey Andrews to deliver the challenge that we had decided upon.

"Listen, Spikey," I said, when I buttonholed him on the borough recreation ground after school one day. "We've got a few scores to settle with you and your bright bunch, for that fast one you pulled on us at Elm Gardens."

Spikey put on his widest grin. "Some people are crazy enough to believe anything!"

I couldn't help smiling a bit myself; after all, there *was* a funny side to it, in spite of everything we'd had to put up with.

"We can take a joke as well as anyone," I went on. "But just at the moment we can't afford to waste time larking about because we've got a big job to do, raising funds for our Great Hall."

"Why not let it fall down? They might build you a proper one then—like ours," he smirked.

I ignored the insult, and said: "I was hoping you chaps might like to help us."

Spikey nearly had hysterics. "What *us*! . . . Help *you*! Nice bunch of Charleys we'd look, going round working our fingers to the bone to save your moth-eaten old dump."

"No, I'm not asking you to do any work. I've got a much better idea." Whereupon I told him about our speedway, and suggested he might like to make up a team of racing cyclists to meet our Sheldrake side on the following Saturday afternoon.

"There'll be a collection, of course," I warned him. "I'm hoping both sides will bring along all the supporters they can lay hands on, to make the meeting a great financial success."

Spikey brooded over the scheme for some moments. Then he said: "Suits me. It'll be a change from mock battles, anyway. What's the prize if we win?"

I hadn't given a thought to that aspect of the matter. "Well—er—how about racing for the flags?" I suggested.

He shook his head. "No jolly fear! If you want to challenge us, it's up to you to dish out a trophy worth racing for."

"I'll see what I can do. Just leave it to me," I said.

It was rather a rash promise, because at the time I hadn't the slightest idea of where I could find a trophy worthy of the great event. On the other hand, I didn't want Spikey to back out, so I decided to take a chance. . . . As things turned out it was well worth it.

Spikey Andrews was as good as his word. On Saturday afternoon he turned up at the Victoria Crescent speedway track with a team of six budding cycle champions and about forty enthusiastic supporters.

We had mustered nearly twice that number of faithful fans, and Boko Phipps, who had charge of the collecting box, danced with delight.

"This lot will be good for at least six pounds—perhaps more, if we can stop them from getting away before I've been round with the box," he said. Then he noticed my thoughtful frown and asked: "What are you looking so fossilized about, Rex? Anything wrong?"

"Not yet, but there may be soon," I answered. "Spikey wants a trophy for the winning team, and what with one thing and another I haven't had a chance to do anything about finding one."

"Tell him not to be such a miserable pot-hunter," said Boko indignantly. "Tell him that prizes will endanger his amateur status. Tell him . . ."

But I didn't get a chance to tell him anything, because at that moment Scuttersthorp and Evans, whom we had appointed marshals of the course, started chivvying the competitors to the starting point for the first race.

We'd agreed that both sides should enter two competitors only for each event, as the track wasn't wide enough to cope with more than four cyclists at a time. Even so, there was precious little elbow-room, and it was clear that overtaking was going to be a somewhat tricky manoeuvre.

The first event was the Six Laps Under Fourteen, which was won in a frenzy of excitement by J. O. Stagg, the hope of the Sheldrake side. He shot ahead right from the start, and had built up a comfortable lead by the time he started on the last lap. In fact, he looked an easy winner, but unfortunately his chain dropped to pieces twenty yards from the finish, and he had to gallop along wheeling his machine for the rest of the way. He nosed past the tape a bare six inches ahead of his Technical opponent!

"Wacko! First win to us!" chanted Boko, rattling the two pennies he'd put in his box to start off the collection.

"Next race! Ten Laps Open!" announced Scuttersthorp. "Andrews and Tucker for the Tech, versus Johnson and Milligan for Sheldrake's."

Spikey looked pretty confident as he sat astride his machine waiting for the start. "You haven't shown me the trophy yet, Milligan," he said. "It'd better be something worth racing for, or there'll be a spot of trouble brewing around these parts before the day's over."

How right he was! . . . But it wasn't the sort of trouble that any of us were expecting.

Alfie Cutforth was starting the race. "On your marks!" he shouted. "Ten seconds to go. . . . Five . . . Four . . . Three . . . Two . . . One . . . *Off!*"

We thrust down heavily on our pedals: the blue riband of the Victoria Crescent cycle-racing track had begun!

Ten laps sounds quite a respectable distance, but in point of fact it was less than a mile on our undersized speedway. For the first hundred yards we jockeyed for position. We couldn't get up speed while we were bunched together, for it was as much as we could do to skid round the bumps and avoid taking a header over the handlebars.

During the second circuit, Jigger worked his way to the front. Then I overtook him two laps later and held on to the lead like grim death. Spikey had been lying third all this while, but as the flag dropped for the last lap he suddenly shot past us—head well down and standing on the pedals.

"Come on, you chronics," he shouted as he flashed by. "I thought you challenged us to a race. What's up —engine trouble?"

Well, I wasn't going to be beaten on the post by S. Andrews, Esq. The time had come for an all-out effort.

I crouched forwards over the handlebars, working up the pace. Jigger tagged on behind me, and the three of us pelted flat-out round the track, heedless of the fact that our tyres might go for six at any moment. Faster and faster we went, leaving the portly Bubblegum further and further behind.

Soon there was less than half a lap to go. We came up to the final bend with Spikey still in the lead—but only just! I was hard on his tail, pulling up foot by foot, and all set to overtake as soon as we were on the straight. He couldn't shake me off, try as he would, so just as I drew level with his back wheel he suddenly swung outwards to stop me from shooting past.

I hadn't a hope of avoiding him. There was a jarring *whoomph-sproing* sort of noise, and we both pancaked with a wallop. Jigger was just behind. He crashed into my back wheel, turned head over heels and landed on top of us.

Then the ground gave way. . . .

Ever so gently it caved in under us in a kind of miniature earthquake, and we slithered out of sight, complete with bikes and a few hundredweight of soil and rubble.

I came to rest about ten feet below ground level; and when I'd unplastered my eyes, the first thing I saw was Spikey's face goggling at me upside down through the frame of his bike.

"Gosh! What's happened? Where are we?" he gasped.

I removed a piece of rusty iron from my chest and looked around.

The daylight was somewhat feeble down there, but in spite of that I could make out the brick walls of a cellar. It was full of junk, too—old dustbins, water-tanks and what-have-you, half buried in earth. Then I spotted Jigger, who'd landed up some yards away astride a long shiny object. It looked like a cylinder of some sort.

"Don't get in a flap, Spikey," I answered. "I think we're in the basement of one of the houses that were here before the war. They should have been filled in by rights, but they seem to have missed this one."

From the other side of the cellar Jigger chimed in: "Didn't you spot the dip in the track? I noticed the earth was shifting a bit the last time we rode over it. I never guessed there was a prefabricated elephant-trap underneath it, though."

By this time some of the spectators had swarmed across the side and were peering down at us from the rim of the crater. "Get back, you chaps," I warned them. "It's all hollow underneath the spot where you're standing. You'll send a lot more stuff down on top of us if you dance about up there."

The spectators retired to a safe distance, and we set about the task of climbing back to ground level.

First we pushed the bicycles out of the hole, as they were nearer the top than we were. Then, just as we were ready to scramble after them, Jigger knocked his foot on the sausage-shaped affair that he'd landed on. . . . It went *boyng!*

"What's that?" Spikey sounded a bit edgy.

"It was me; I kicked something," said Jigger. "Sounds like metal. Listen!" And he did it again—*boyng!*

I ploughed my way across to have a look. I couldn't see the ends of the object because they were covered in soil, but the middle part reflected a patch of light from the hole above our heads. I put out my hand and felt the round, smooth surface.

"What is it?" asked Spikey.

"I'm not sure," I told him. "It's a metal cylinder of some sort. In fact, it looks to me like an unexploded bomb."

Exit Andrews! *Swoosh*—just like that!

One moment he was standing behind me, and the next there was a slither of loose earth and Spikey had scrambled out of the cellar, retrieved his bike, and was pedalling away from the target area as though he was trying to crash the sound barrier.

I looked at Jigger and said: "I can quite see Spikey's point. *If* that's an unexploded bomb, and *if* it decides to go off . . ."

"Well, don't hang about making speeches," he broke in. "Let's get out quickly. Curiosity killed the cat."

He climbed up the earthy slope; and while I was waiting my turn to follow I took another glance at the sinister-looking cylinder. A small metal plate caught my eye, so I scratched away a handful of earth and examined the object more thoroughly. I wanted to be quite sure, you see.

"Come on, Rex."

I looked up to see Jigger peering down from the top of our little crater. He gave me a hand to help me out, and then we picked up our bikes and rode across the cycle track to the pavement.

You'd never believe the hoo-hah that was going on when we got there. Spikey Andrews was waving his arms round like a paddle-steamer out of control, shooing everyone away from the ruins.

"Get back, get back—it's not safe!" he was shouting. "There's an unexploded bomb in one of the basements."

"Listen, Spikey," I began.

"Everybody clear off—right away out of this street," he went on. "Some of those bombs can be set off by vibration, and we've just brought down about ten tons of rubbish on it. All get away out of range; and no charging about—the slightest movement is liable to set the fuse going!"

He demonstrated how to tread delicately, wheeling his bike and walking on tip-toe like some elephantine ballerina.

Well, Spikey's news bulletin cleared the deck right enough, and nobody would listen to me when I tried to stem the panic with a dose of cool, calm reason. In two bats of an eyelid teams and spectators had scuttled away round the corner, to await the big bang at a safe distance.

At the tail end of the flying column was Boko Phipps, rattling his collecting-box in a half-hearted attempt to save the financial situation.

"This is frantic," he groaned as he passed me. "They're all bolting off without paying. I've only collected a few coppers so far—and I've a pretty shrewd idea that one of *those* was a foreign coin!"

"Too bad," I consoled him. "And they can't even say they're not getting their money's worth, with all this hoo-hah laid on for their entertainment."

Jigger and I were the last to leave the Crescent. As

we followed the crowd round the corner, Jigger said: "Oughtn't we to do something about it, Rex?"

I shrugged my shoulders. "What more can we do? Spikey seems to have got everything nicely taped, so we'd better let him get on with it. . . . I'm going home to my tea."

THE UNEXPLODED RUMOUR

I WAS just settling down to my week-end prep an hour later, when Jigger came swinging up the garden path. He caught sight of me through the dining-room window and called out: "Hey, Rex, heard the latest? Spikey's been to the police and there's no end of a flap going on. They've closed the Crescent and they're going to start evacuating the houses in the streets all round. Come and have a look."

I abandoned my prep, and together we hurried back to the bombed site, where we found warning notices posted up left, right and centre. *Danger, Unexploded Bomb* greeted us in large red letters on a white board as soon as we turned the corner. Policemen were guarding the barricades which had been erected at each end of the crescent, and various odd characters were trotting hither and thither with sandbags.

I decided that this particular caper had gone far enough. "We'll have to tell them, Jig," I said with a sigh.

He looked surprised. "Tell them? Tell them *what*?"

"Well, it's like this. I had another squint at that

bomb while you were climbing out of the cellar. I found it had got a metal plate with instructions screwed on the side."

Jigger goggled in wide-eyed astonishment. "Wow! Instructions! In German, I suppose?"

"No, they were in English. They said: *It is important to ensure that the water is running freely before igniting the gas.*"

"Uh!"

"In other words, Spikey's unexploded bomb happens to be an old-fashioned bathroom geyser."

"What! . . . Are you sure?"

"Of course I'm sure. I was going to tell everyone not to get the wind up, but he was creating such a hoo-hah that no one would listen to me. I'd no idea the police would take it seriously, though."

Jigger curled up with mirth. Then he pulled himself together and said: "We'd better go and explain before things get any worse, hadn't we?"

So we pushed our way through the crowd milling round the policeman. "Excuse me, but there's been a bit of a bish," I told the P.C. "That thing in the crater is perfectly safe. It can't possibly explode. I've been down the hole and seen it."

The constable was in no mood to suffer fools gladly, or to waste time listening to the burblings of a well-meaning half-wit.

"Oh, yes," he replied in tones heavy with disbelief. "You're a bit of an expert on explosives, I take it. You can tell whether a bomb will go off just by looking at it, I suppose!"

"Well, no. But this isn't a bomb at all. It's just an old brass geyser. I'm not pulling your leg—honestly."

"Very interesting, I'm sure," he said scathingly. "All the same, I think we'll take proper precautions, until someone who knows what he's talking about has had a look at it."

I made one more effort to make him see reason, but I was wasting my breath. He'd been given orders not to let anyone past the barrier, and nothing I said would convince him that Spikey had rootled up the biggest mare's-nest since flying saucers.

The people I felt sorry for were the unfortunate householders in the adjoining streets, who were half expecting to see their premises blown skyhigh at any moment.

"I reckon we ought to do something before they evacuate the houses," I said to Jigger. "If we could *show* them it was only a geyser, they'd all feel a lot happier."

"Maybe they would," Jigger agreed. "But how are we going to do that, if they won't let us near the thing?"

It was hopeless trying to get past the policemen, so we scouted round the other three roads which bordered the site. There were warning notices all over the place, but at last we found an alleyway leading to the Crescent between the back gardens of the ruined houses. There was a rope barrier across the entrance, but no one was guarding it.

I looked up and down the road. . . . The coast was clear! So we ducked under the rope, scurried down the alley, and came out on the ruins. Then we slipped across to the crater, slithered down to the bottom, and set to work.

It didn't take long to shift the loose earth from the ends of the bogus bomb and ease it clear of the rubbish. We examined the object with keen interest.

Frankly, I'd never seen such an ancient crock of a geyser before in my life. It looked as though it had been made in the reign of Alfred the Great: and there were so many taps and tubes and lengths of brass piping leading nowhere in particular, that I doubt if any bomb disposal expert would have known where to start work!

Jigger laughed till he was weak.

"Perhaps this was the contraption that wrecked the house," he suggested fatuously. "Perhaps someone lit the gas before the water was running freely, and when it went pop everyone thought there was a raid on. We should have brought the Staggers with us. This old relic would have kept him happy for hours!"

Together we heaved the geyser out of the cellar, carried it across to the pavement and marched proudly towards the barricade at the end of the Crescent.

Our friend the constable spotted us while we were some distance away. His head jerked forward and his eyes bulged with bewilderment.

"Hey! What are you doing there? And what's that you're carrying?" he shouted.

"Don't worry. It's only ye guaranteed bomb-shell," I explained, as we came up and dropped the clanking relic at his feet.

The P.C. didn't know what to say; and as for the crowd milling about on the "safe" side of the barrier —well, they couldn't have been more surprised if we'd just landed from Mars by rocket.

Most of the spectators from the afternoon's sports meeting had come back to see the excitement. Boko was there, with Alfie and Stagg and Bubblegum. . . . And Spikey Andrews was in the front row, of course!

Spikey stared at his "bomb" as though it was the ghost of Hamlet's father. Then, scarlet with shamefaced embarrassment, he edged his way to the back of the crowd and disappeared.

The next few minutes were somewhat hectic—what with explaining matters to the policeman and answering his questions. But when at last the hoo-hah had died down, Boko said: "What are you going to do with the geyser, Rex?"

"I don't know. Chuck it back in the basement, I suppose."

It was then that Jigger had one of his rare bursts of genius. "We *won't* chuck it back," he declared. "We can still use the track if we keep clear of hollow basements, can't we?"

I nodded.

"Well then. Here's the famous trophy we can present to the winning side—if Spikey's willing to have another go."

"Oh, he'll be willing right enough," said Boko. "His name will be Mud up at the Tech when the news gets round he was frightened by a geyser. Just give him half a chance to restore his reputation and he'll take it like a shot—you mark my words."

Boko was right. By the following morning, when the shock had worn off, no one was more anxious to stage another contest than yours truly, S. Andrews.

But once again our plans were thwarted. The scare at Victoria Crescent hit the headlines in the local press, and the authorities decided it was high time the place was put to some good purpose. So when we went back there a few days later, we found corporation workmen busily engaged in turning the site into an official car park. The foreman chivvied us away in no uncertain terms, and even threatened to report us for trespassing on council property.

"Doesn't that just show you how everything's against us?" moaned Boko as we tottered away from the bombed site, shaking our heads sadly over the shattering blows of Fate. "I go to all the trouble of thinking out the most brilliant money-making scheme in history—and how much do we get out of it? . . . Nine pence in coppers and a ten-franc piece!"

There was no doubt that misfortune was dogging our footsteps. The second of our water-tight schemes had sprung a nasty leak. Our only hope now was the third, and last, item on the agenda—the purveying of high-class jumble.

"The sooner Rex gets cracking with his scheme the better," Jigger observed as we reached the corner of the Crescent. "And let's hope nothing comes unstuck. It's our last chance to rake in the shekels, don't forget."

We exchanged sheepish grins. The task of raising thirty pounds was proving to be more difficult than we had imagined. Perhaps there was some knack in amassing vast wealth that we hadn't quite tumbled to!

"We'll make a special effort this time, anyway," I declared. "I vote we rope in all the chaps who helped us build the cycle track, and send them on a house-to-house tour of the district, collecting all the stuff they can lay their hands on."

"What sort of stuff?" queried Boko doubtfully.

"Well—er, priceless merchandise, if they can find any; if not, any old junk will do for a kick-off. We shall want all we can get."

"And where are we going to hold this fabulous sale? Strikes me we shall need a place the size of the Albert Hall," Boko persisted.

"Not quite," I assured him. "I shall go and see the Head-hunter tomorrow and ask him if we can use the gym. After all, it's for the good of the school, isn't it!"

The Head-hunter was all in favour of the jumble

sale when I went along to his study after lunch next day and made my tactful request for permission. It was most encouraging, he told me, to see such enthusiasm and initiative, and to feel that the whole school was working together in a common cause. . . . A jumble sale? Splendid idea, splendid! . . . Permission to hold it in the gynasium? . . . H'm *Not* so splendid.

There followed the sharp intake of breath, the pursing of the lips and the raising of the pained eyebrow. Even in a worthy cause the Head-hunter had no intention of allowing the gym to be turned into a second-hand junk shop.

He brooded over the matter for a few moments, and then moved an amendment. "I hardly think, Milligan, that the gymnasium is quite the place to stage a function of this kind. On the other hand, I see no reason why you shouldn't hold it in the hut used by the Hobbies Club. That, surely, would be equally suitable for your purpose."

"Yes, sir. . . . Thank you, sir."

Jigger Johnson was waiting for me just outside the door of the great man's study.

"Any luck, Rex?" he inquired.

"Yes, rather. We can use the Hobbies hut. The old boy didn't jib at all. Must have been those prunes we had for lunch that put him in a decent mood, because—"

I broke off suddenly. Jigger's eyes were flashing a message of warning, his lips mouthing silent alarm.

I glanced round. . . . The unlatched door had swung open and the Head-hunter was standing just inside, listening to my comments with keen interest.

"Sorry, sir," I mumbled, pink to the ears with confusion.

He froze me with an icy stare.

"I can assure you, Milligan, that the decisions I am called upon to make are seldom influenced by the excellence of the fare provided for school lunch."

"Yes, sir! . . . I mean, no, sir! Sorry, sir."

I closed the door properly this time, and as I did so I noticed that the frozen stare had thawed, and that a faint smile was playing round the corners of the headmaster's mouth. Not a bad old stick, really, our H.M., I reflected. But this time I didn't speak my thoughts aloud.

DR. STALLYBONE

We wasted no time in organizing our gangs of amateur junk collectors. After tea the next day, Jigger set out in one direction with a squad of foragers, while I took the Staggers and Alfie Cutforth to help me in my search for salvage in a different part of the suburb.

It was a slow business, because we had to cool our heels on every other doorstep while friendly householders rummaged through their attics; and even so, most of them asked us to call back later when they would have had more time to sort out their contributions. But we persevered, and after a couple of hours' hard graft we'd collected more jumble than we could carry in comfort.

Most of the merchandise consisted of boots, books, kitchen utensils and out-dated garments, all showing signs of wear and tear. But as well as these we had acquired a rickety bath-chair, a wireless condenser, a cabinet gramophone minus most of its works, and an ear-trumpet.

The Staggers was delighted. His inventive brain sizzled with ideas for transforming the gramophone into a portable radiogram by mounting it on the bath-chair, with the ear-trumpet built in as a loudspeaker. It was all we could do to restrain him from starting work on the project there and then.

"Our job is to collect things for the jumble sale—not to waste time constructing unworkable gadgets," I reminded him. "We've got nearly as much stuff as we can manage now, so I vote we try one more house, and then call it a day."

"Thank goodness," muttered Alfie. "I feel no end of a fool traipsing round with an armful of saucepans and moth-eaten bowler hats—to say nothing of having this coal scuttle slung round my neck like a nosebag."

We had stopped for a short rest in front of a large detached house in a quiet, residential road.

"This looks a likely sort of place," I remarked, as I led my team in through the gate and set my burdens down on the doorstep. . . . Then I pressed the bell.

At once a frenzied yelping and yapping broke out on the far side of the door. Judging by the noise, at least six dogs of varying size and lung-power had taken umbrage at our approach, and were expressing their feelings at full volume. The squeaky barks of the smaller animals mingled with the baritone baying of the larger breeds to form an ear-splitting chorus of disapproval.

With a guilty start, I removed my finger from the electric bell-push; but instead of springing back to its normal position the wretched button remained firmly jammed in its socket, and the bell went on ringing,

"Wow! What a ghastly shemozzle," exclaimed Alfie. "Can't you do something to stop it?"

"That's what I'm trying to do, but the beastly button's got stuck!" I had to shout to make myself heard above the general uproar.

"Let me have a shot," Stagg volunteered. He produced his penknife and inserted the blade into the bell socket in an attempt to release the button. But it was no use: the point of the blade snapped off short at the first attempt. And all the time the shrilling of the bell and the baying of the hounds went on without pause.

"This is frantic," I groaned. "Whatever will they say when they come to open the door!"

"Whatever they say we won't hear it with this racket going on," Alfie bawled back at me. "I vote we skip it while the going's good."

"No jolly fear. We'll have to stick it out now. We can't go ringing at front door bells and running away."

The barks and the bell continued to shatter the peace of the evening for what seemed an eternity, though in point of fact it couldn't have been more than a couple of minutes.

Then a new noise was added to the orchestra, as from beyond the door we heard the clanking of keys, the rattling of chains and the withdrawing of bolts.

"They're not taking any chances with burglars," I remarked. "They've got the place rigged up like a fortress. Goodness knows what'll happen if—"

At that moment the front door opened and a Pekinese dog came catapulting over the threshold with the force of a fighter pilot on an ejector-seat. Close on its heels came a poodle in just as much of a hurry, followed by a mixed canine assortment who streaked out too fast for me to get them properly in focus.

The hounds took no notice of us. Barking and yelping, they tore through the gate and out into the road; while at the tail end of the procession cantered a middle-aged lady in a pinafore, waving her arms at the fleeing animals in a frantic effort to halt their flight.

"Stop them! Stop them!" she called, hopping up and down in agitation: whereupon we abandoned our jumble on the doorstep and pounded off in the wake of the dogs.

It took us about ten minutes to round up the pack When we'd done so, we staggered back to the house bearing the smaller animals in our arms and chivvying the larger ones along with encouraging cries.

The party in the pinafore greeted the returning horde with beams and smiles, patting, stroking and *Good dog*ing left, right and centre. This caused a further outbreak of barks, and as the electric bell was still ringing at maximum volume, conversation was not easy.

Mrs. Pinafore turned to me and mouthed some remark which was carried away in the swirl of sound.

"What did you say?" I yelled back.

Her lips moved again, but no words reached me. So I seized the ear-trumpet from the doorstep, and plugged in the hearing-end to my left ear in the approved manner.

"Try again!" I shouted.

She took a deep breath and bawled down the trumpet with the full force of her lungs. . . . As she did so, the dogs ceased barking, the bell stopped as if by magic, and the only sound that broke the stillness was the strident voice of Mrs. Pinafore demanding to know if I was a trifle hard of hearing.

I lowered the trumpet, to see Stagg turning away from the bell-push. "There you are, that's stopped it," he announced.

"Jolly good! How did you do it?"

"I applied strictly scientific methods and made a

slight mechanical adjustment," he said importantly. "Or to put it in non-technical language, I gave the thing a biff and the button popped back into place!"

Mrs. Pinafore was eyeing us suspiciously. "What is it you've come about?" she asked, shooing the bounding hounds into the house and closing the door on them.

"We just came to see if you'd got any jumble," I explained. Frankly, I thought it sounded rather a feeble excuse for creating such a large-scale disturbance—even though it was *her* dogs and *her* door bell that were mostly to blame.

Mrs. Pinafore didn't think much of the excuse, either.

"It's no good asking me—I'm only the housekeeper," she replied tartly. "And you can't go bothering the doctor—he's resting. Or rather, he *was* resting before you started making all that noise."

"I'm sorry," I apologized.

"So I should think! You've no business to come worrying a scientific gentleman like Dr. Stallybone with a lot of nonsense about jumble sales. He's far too busy with his research work and suchlike to bother about stupid things like that."

The Staggers' eyes lit up in sudden hope. "Do you mean to say the owner of this house is a *scientist*?" he breathed reverently.

"Of course he is. Very well known, too, so they tell me. If you know anything about science you must have heard of Dr. Stallybone, surely?"

"Oh . . . ah . . . yes, of course. . . . Dr. Stallybone!"

The Staggers nodded in a knowing manner. It was clear to me that he had never heard of the learned Dr. S. in his life; but, as a budding scientist himself, he wasn't going to admit the fact. He began to fish for further information.

"Let me see now. Isn't he the expert on atomic physics and nuclear fission?" he asked.

This time it was Mrs. Pinafore who was out of her depth, but as an official of the great man's household she seemed reluctant to confess that she hadn't a clue as to what Stagg was talking about. So she passed it off by mumbling: "I daresay you're right. Both of them, I shouldn't wonder."

"Well, fancy that!" The would-be inventor beamed from ear to ear. "Gosh, I wish I could meet him. I dabble a bit in that sort of thing myself, you know. Mind you, I'm not in the top grade myself—at least, not yet. But *one* day—"

At that moment the front door opened again and a tall, thin character in a hairy tweed suit and bifocal glasses wandered out to see what all the commotion was in aid of.

"What *is* going on out here?" he inquired plaintively.

"It's quite all right, Dr. Stallybone. Just some boys collecting for a jumble," quoth Mrs. Pinafore.

Dr. Stallybone! So this was the great man in person! Stagg gazed at his fellow-scientist in awe and wonder, and even Alfie Cutforth looked pleased at finding himself in the presence of the famous.

I had a feeling I had seen the worthy doctor before, though for a moment I couldn't place him. Then I remembered. . . . He was the vague pedestrian who had been puzzled by Boko's bird-warbler just before our last battle with the Tech. Now he seemed equally baffled at the sight of the jumble strewn over his front doorstep.

"What are all these things doing here?" he asked.

"I never ordered them. There must be some mistake. Take them back to the shop and tell them—"

"You don't understand, Doctor. They're *collecting* this stuff, not delivering it," the housekeeper pointed out.

"Yes, we want all we can get," Alfie chimed in. "We're doing it in support of our Great Hall at school, because the roof's in an unsafe condition, you see, sir."

Dr. Stallybone looked more nonplussed than ever. He waved an arm vaguely at the gramophone wobbling precariously on the bath-chair.

"But, my dear boy, these things are no earthly use. They wouldn't support the roof of a chicken house—let alone a school hall!"

Dr. Stallybone may have had a first-class brain so far as the mysteries of science were concerned, but he seemed a trifle slow in the uptake over every-day matters like rummage sales. However, I managed to make him understand that we didn't propose to prop up the Great Hall roof with pilllars of jumble: and when at last he understood what we'd come for, he fairly bristled with eagerness to help the cause.

"Why, of course, let me think now," he mused. "I'm sure if I look carefully in the box-room I shall find some useful ornaments, or suitable *bric-à-brac*."

"Suitable *what-à-which*?" queried Alfie, out of his depth.

"Odds and ends," translated Dr. Stallybone. "Let us go indoors and see."

He led the way into the hall and then through to the kitchen, with Stagg hopping at his heels and hoping for a privileged peep behind the scenes. He's keenly space-minded, is the Staggers, and he looked about him with excited interest as though half expecting to see space-helmets on the hat-stand or even flying saucers on the plate-rack.

He was unlucky. We saw no astonishing headgear apart from the doctor's ageing cloth cap. Neither were there any saucers actually in flight; though we heard one or two skimming about on the scullery floor, where the dogs were polishing off a tasty snack provided by Mrs. Pinafore.

"Wait here and I'll see what I can find," said Dr. Stallybone. He disappeared up the back stairs and returned a few minutes later bearing a barometer, an old leather despatch-case and a wall-map showing Europe at the time of the Franco-Prussian war.

Stagg looked a little disappointed. He had obviously been hoping for a Geiger-counter, or a few samples of uranium. However, we accepted the gifts with grateful thanks, picked our way through the swarm of dogs, and set off on the return journey.

It was dark by this time, and the going was slow as we were cluttered to the eyebrows with merchandise of every description.

"Phew! I've just about had enough of this lark," moaned Alfie after we'd gone a few hundred yards. "It's at least a mile and a half back to school, and I bet we find the place locked up when we get there."

"No, we shan't. I've had a word with the school-keeper," I told him. "All the same, I'm beginning to wish we'd got some form of transport laid on, because—"

At that moment a noise like a pneumatic drill was wafted down the road towards us, and a few seconds later an incredibly ancient car rattled past, screeched on its brakes and came to rest beside a street lamp.

Our spirits rose. We knew that car . . . We knew the driver, too!

"Wacko! It's the Frizzer! I wonder if he'll give us a lift," I exclaimed.

Mr. Frisby, *alias* the Frizzer, is our modern languages master at Sheldrake's. He's a large, hearty type with a booming voice, a vast moustache and none of the quiet dignity of the average usher. His vintage car, which he calls "Old Faithful", is something out of the ordinary, too. In appearance it's a bright red, rickety contraption which looks like a mobile incubator with a built-in engine.

I'm not saying a word against ye chariot, mind you. They made good cars in the 1920's, and they made them to last. And Old Faithful *has* lasted—more or less. There's none of this modern craze for synchro-mesh gears and fluid flywheels about her, either. She's got personality and character, instead. She rumbles along on her narrow, spindly wheels at a deafening fifteen m.p.h. whenever she feels in the mood, and stops for a short rest when she thinks she's gone far enough.

"You boys want a lift?" boomed Mr. Frisby, in tones which carried the length of the road.

"Yes please, sir! Thank you very much, sir!"

He eyed our bulky burdens in surprise. "What's all this—moving house?"

"No, sir; it's for the jumble sale we're holding in aid of the Great Hall," I explained.

"Good show," said the Frizzer. "I should say you've got enough there to equip an armoured column. Put it in the back, and climb in on top."

Stagg looked doubtful. "Are you sure it won't be putting too much strain on the springs, sir?"

"*Springs?* What makes you think this car has springs, Stagg, eh?" The Frizzer exclaimed; and then roared with laughter at his little joke. That's just like

Mr. Frisby: he's devoted to Old Faithful, of course, but he *can* see the funny side of things.

We set to work, loading the car till the axles groaned. Floor and seats were packed tight, and the cargo rose as high as the flapping hood before the last of our bulky objects was safely stowed. The bath-chair was lashed to the running-board: the Frizzer refused to tow it behind the car as we couldn't fix it up with a rear light and number-plates.

"Phew! That's the lot, thank goodness," panted Alfie, when everything was in place. "The bulkheads are bulging like blinko, but I reckon they'd just about hold till we get back to school."

Then the three of us climbed aboard and packed ourselves in wherever we could find a square inch of foothold.

"All set? Hold tight, then—we're off!" boomed the Frizzer. He heaved at a wire dangling from the dash-board. . . . And then let go with a sudden gasp of anguish.

"Anything the matter, sir?"

"No, no, nothing serious. I got an electric shock from the self-starter, that's all. Must be a short circuit somewhere."

We were not surprised. "Bad luck, sir. Will you be able to mend it?"

"It's hardly worth the bother," Mr. Frisby observed. "If I leave it alone it'll probably cure itself in time. That's what I like about this car—there's never a dull moment."

"She'll start all right with the crank, won't she, sir?" I asked.

"Yes, yes, of course. But unfortunately the starting handle is underneath the back seat, which you've carefully battened down with half a ton of miscellaneous refuse. I think it would be quicker if you all hopped out and gave me a push."

"I might have known it!" Alfie muttered bitterly under his breath.

And not without reason! The royal and ancient sport of *Pushing Old Faithful* is one of the things you learn to get used to when you've been at the Grammar for a term or two. There's nothing fairy-like about her weight, you see; and if you can imagine yourself forming a rugger scrum against a pack of yaks with their hoofs dug well in, you'll get some idea of what it's like to shove the Frizzer's rattling relic along the highway.

With many an inward groan and muffled *tut-tut* we disentangled ourselves and clambered on to the road. Then we put our heads down and pushed.

Under this treatment Old Faithful *has* been known to start chugging after the first hundred yards. But this wasn't one of her good days. . . . Gasping and straining, we struggled along for furlong after furlong, while Mr. Frisby sat comfortably in the driving seat, urging us on to greater efforts.

"She'll start any minute now!" he prophesied after the first quarter mile. And at the half-mile he said: "She's just a little sluggish this evening. Never mind! Press on, chaps, eh?"

We pressed on. . . . And when at last the mighty motor roared to life we found we were so near the school gates that it wasn't worth while climbing aboard.

"Cor! What a mouldy chizz. I didn't bargain for this carry-on!" complained Alfie as we marched alongside Old Faithful like funeral mutes accompanying a hearse. "The Frizzer offers us a lift to save us the fag of carting the stuff, and then makes us walk the whole way, pushing him and his old grid-iron as though we needed the exercise!"

"Bear up, Cutforth," I encouraged him. "There's even harder work ahead of us before we reach our thirty pound target."

I never spoke a truer word!

BARGAIN IN GENT'S OUTFITTING

ACCORDING to my diary, October 25th is an important date in English history as it commemorates the Battle of Agincourt. From now on, it also marks the anniversary of the Form 4 jumble sale.

We chose the Saturday before half term on which to hold the great event. Zero hour was 3 p.m., but ever since breakfast time the Hobbies hut on the junior quad had been seething with organizers in shirt-sleeves, sorting out the stock and sticking price labels on to everything within reach. When most of the hard work was finished, Alfie Cutforth arrived, wearing a home-made armlet marked *Store Detective.*

"I'm going to keep my eye on the customers," he declared, frowning with self-importance. "There's usually a bit of a shemozzle when the crowd rushes the doors at the kick-off, and it's then that the hardened criminals will start snaffling the goods from under our very noses."

Jigger paused in the act of chalking 25p on Dr. Stallybone's despatch case. "I shouldn't think anyone would be so mean," he objected.

"Huh! Don't you believe it! We held a rummage sale at our church hall last year, and do you know what? One crafty specimen worked her way along the table 'accidentally' knocking piles of clothes and stuff on to the floor."

"I don't see anything criminal in that."

"Ah, but she had a confederate crawling along under the tables keeping pace with her, and picking the things up as they dropped. Came out the other end and fairly bursting with size eight gym-shoes and pull-overs. You never saw such a bundle of booty!"

"All right, then. Alfie; you keep tabs on the clients," I agreed. "But if I were you I wouldn't advertise what I was doing."

"Trust me!" he said with a knowing smirk. "I shan't let them know I've got my eye on them."

I pointed to his armband. "How about that for giving the game away?"

Alfie's hand shot to his mouth in sudden realization. "Fossilized fish-hooks! I never thought of that. Thanks for the tip, Milligan!" He removed the tell-tale label and wandered off to plan further security arrangements.

The news of the sale had spread far and wide, and at two o'clock a crowd began to gather outside the school gates. From time to time we popped our heads out to see how long the queue was growing; and shortly before the doors were due to open, I decided to boost the publicity still further by displaying a notice outside the gate. So I borrowed a blackboard from Classroom 4, carried it out into the street, and started chalking:

TODAY!
JUMBLE SALE!
COLOSSAL BARGAINS!
ROLL UP AND SPEND YOUR MONEY IN A
WORTHY CAUSE!

As I stepped back to admire the effect of my artistry, I almost trod on the toes of a small, foreign-looking man with curly black hair and a stubbly blue chin, who was studying the announcement with keen interest. He accepted my apologies with a beaming smile and then asked: "Please, what means this jumble sale?"

At least, that's a free translation of his inquiry. What he actually *said* was: "Pliss, ward mince diss chompell sell?"

We've got a fair sprinkling of foreigners in our suburb. Some of them are refugees who've been here for years, but even so they haven't all learned to get their tongues round the more difficult words of our language. This chap was anything but fluent. His accent was so marked that I had to ask him to repeat what he'd said before I could decide whether he was talking in English or his mother tongue. However, I caught the drift at the second attempt, and did my best to provide a lucid explanation.

"Well, a jumble sale is a place where you—er—where you buy jumble!" I said, somewhat inadequately.

The little man waved his hand at the queue. "Diss pipples all hop to buy a chompell? 'Ow many chompells for each pipple?"

It took me some while to explain that the people hoping to buy jumble could have as much of it as they could afford. He seemed satisfied with this and passed on to the next item on the agenda.

" 'Ow is diss wordy cows?" he inquired earnestly.

That had me guessing for a moment, until I saw he was reading the last line of my notice on the blackboard.

"Oh, ah . . . Worthy cause—yes, I see what you mean," I exclaimed as light dawned. How could I put it plainly? "A worthy cause is a—Well, it's a very good thing!"

The explanation sounded feeble to me, but the little dark man nodded in understanding.

" 'Ere you sell a good t'ing, yes? 'Ere I find wordy cows, no?'

"No!" I said firmly.

But it didn't deter him. He joined himself on to the tail of the queue, anxious not to miss whatever entertainment was being laid on for his benefit. I think he was under the impression that he was going to see an exhibition of some sort.

I went back into the Hobbies hut to make sure that all the salesmen were on their toes, ready to cope with the big rush at opening time.

"Five minutes to go," I said to Scuttersthorp, who was guarding the doors. "There's a whole mob of people outside in the street. Don't let them in till the school clock strikes the hour."

In one corner of the hut I spied Boko Phipps, who was looking after our tasteful display of ladies' hats. He was entertaining his fellow salesmen by picking out the more repulsive samples from his stock and trying them on to see what he looked like. In order to show off each model to its best advantage he contorted his face into ghastly grimaces and then pranced up and down the room in clumsy parody of a mannequin.

"Break it up, chaps. Everyone to action stations! The balloon's due to go up at any minute now," I told them. Then I noticed that Staggers, who was supposed to be in charge of the odd-gadget department, was mooching about at the wrong end of the room, clutching the old despatch case which Dr. Stallybone had given us.

"Hey! What are you doing with that case? It's

supposed to be on that table next to the boots and shoes," I pointed out.

"I was only having a look at it. I thought it would be rather a decent thing to keep my private papers in," he defended himself. Then, hopefully, he woffled on: "I see it's priced at twenty-five pence, but if you'd be willing to knock ten pence off . . ."

"It's a tempting offer, Staggers, but I've no time for bargaining at the moment," I said, prising the despatch case from his grasp. "If the thing's not sold during the afternoon you can have it, but we can't afford to make any reductions just yet."

"Oh, but look here—just a minute," he objected as I made off with the mouldering leather object in tow.

"Can't stop now! See me about it later." I strode the length of the hut and restored the despatch case to its rightful place.

Then a thought struck me. It was more than likely that a vague, absent-minded genius like Dr. Stallybone wouldn't have thought to look inside his despatch case before handing it over. Supposing he had left something inside? Better have a look and see! I snapped back the catch and turned the case upside down over the table . . .

I was right! Half-a-dozen sheets of typewritten paper fluttered out. They were fastened together with a paper clip and looked like notes of some sort, for I could see headings and numbered paragraphs.

But I didn't look at them long enough to take in what they were all about, because at once my eye was caught by a thicker sheet of notepaper which fell out separately from the main sheaf, and came to rest face upwards on the table.

I goggled at the typewritten heading in stupefied

amazement. Surely it couldn't *really* mean what it said!

Jigger was standing just behind me, putting the finishing touches to our display of potted plants and cracked crockery.

"I say, Jig, come and see what I've found," I called excitedly. He abandoned his wares and came hurrying to join me. Together we absorbed the contents of the typewritten page.

Atomic Research Commission, it was headed; and underneath that it said: *Top Secret. Circulation restricted to "H" Group Research Personnel. For security reasons this memorandum is not to be removed from Admin. Room M/47, or the data divulged to unauthorized persons.*

Then came a formula which went something like this:

Section IX "ATIR" Scheme
Cyclotronically bombard 20 *mg U*238 *using* D_2O *screens.*
At 5 *Mev* (*I zero*) *neutron chain reaction continues*:

$$U238+XN+Io=U235+\beta+\epsilon$$

$$\text{When } A\beta=\frac{(my)}{(mx)}+\gamma$$

$$\text{Thus, } XN= \ldots.$$

Well, not having a photographic brain, I can't exactly remember what *XN* equalled, but I *do* remember that the rest of the formula went to town in a big way with the cube root of a fearsome row of figures and symbols which occupied the rest of the page. A footnote at the end of the formula said: *N.B. β must not be allowed to exceed the above specification without special precautions being taken.*

I don't know whether the aforesaid gobbledeygook means very much to you: it certainly didn't to me. But then, I'm not one of these bulging-browed mathematicians; and I wouldn't know how to set about constructing an atom bomb, even if you handed me the ingredients in a pudding basin with a sprig of holly on the top.

All the same, the words made sense even though the symbols didn't, and it was pretty clear that we'd got hold of a private document that ought to be under lock and key. At first glance it seemed the sort of thing that any mysterious foreign agent would willingly give his false whiskers to possess.

"Golly! How did this get here?" Jigger breathed in puzzled wonder.

"It dropped out of Dr. Stallybone's despatch case with these other papers," I explained as I pinned the formula to the typewritten sheaf.

"I've heard of absent-minded professors but this is carrying the thing too far. He could be prosecuted for leaving valuable secrets like this lying about."

"What had we better do, then?"

"I'll take care of this little lot till after the sale," I said, slipping the papers into the pocket of my jacket which was hanging on a peg on the wall. "Then as soon as it's over I'll go straight round to Dr. Stallybone's house and . . ."

The school clock struck three at that moment. Scuttersthorp opened the doors—and then leapt for safety as the first wild rush of frenzied jumble shoppers came charging in like a herd of stampeding wildebeeste thundering across the veldt. They advanced down the room with shopping bags at the ready, and the steely glint of the bargain-hunter shining in their eyes.

Most of our amateur salesmen had already taken

cover behind their barricades of stock, but a few unfortunate specimens who were still out in the open found themselves swept sideways like mosquitoes struck by the insect-deflector of a fast-moving car.

In a matter of seconds the tables were surrounded by seasoned remnant snatchers, sorting through the slumber-wear, ferreting through the footwear and churning up our neatly folded piles of household linen to see what they could find among the lower layers.

Boko's display of feminine headgear was tossed about like confetti as customers tried on one model after another. From time to time a tug-o'-war would break out, as two or more rival purchasers grabbed the same hat at the same time: and then the air would be filled with portions of millinery parachuting down to earth after being hurled aloft in the heat of the battle.

Turmoil and confusion seethed in all parts of the room. . . . At one point in the proceedings, a trestle table stacked high with books collapsed under the pressure of the crowd, burying the customers under the *débris*, and the salesmen under the customers.

A little later on, I caught sight of my small foreign friend wedged tightly in a slow-moving stream of buyers. He was clutching an aspidistra under one arm and a frying-pan under the other, and was beaming and smiling at everyone within range. Now that he had found out what a "chompell sel" was like, he seemed to approve of the function. From the look on his face you'd have thought he'd discovered the ideal way of spending a quiet Saturday afternoon.

And yet, despite the chaos, business was brisk. The customers were in too much of a hurry to haggle over the prices, as they were eager to get on to the next department before the best bargains had been snapped up. As the minutes sped by, so the money flowed in, and the chink of coins was as music in the Hon. Treasurer's ear.

"Just look at them all digging into their purses," Jigger exclaimed happily, as soon as we could spare enough breath for conversation. "Old Boko's left-hand pocket is so weighed down with the cash he's raking in for those gruesome hats that he's walking about with a limp!"

The Store Detective forced his way towards us through the crowd. "Got change for a pound note?" he asked. "I've been roped in to help Evans and Clarke in the men's clothing department. They're so rushed off their feet they don't know which way to turn. Who'd have thought a jumble sale would be so popular!"

He charged off into the crowd with the change that Jigger thrust upon him. It was odd to think that Cutforth, who had started off as a bitter opponent of the Great Hall fund, should now be one of its most zealous supporters!

By half-past three the first mad rush was over, and we settled down to steady business. There was so much stock to dispose of, and so many people flitting from table to table, that it was nearly five o'clock before the last satisfied customer tottered away from the precincts with her armful of bargains.

"All bring your takings up to the Hon. Treasurer—*i.e.* me," Jigger announced to the sagging salesmen. "It's time to tot up and prepare a balance sheet."

"We haven't done too badly, have we?" said Boko, pouring a cascade of coins on to the auditor's table. "You should have seen the rush for that ghastly headgear. I couldn't take the money fast enough. I'd sold the lot inside twenty minutes!"

"Except the one you're wearing," I pointed out.

"Eh!" Boko gaped like a goldfish. His hand flew to his head and tore off the absurd pimple of millinery that had been perching there throughout the proceedings. "Gosh, have I been wearing this monstrosity all this time?" he cried aghast.

"Ever since your mannequin parade before the sale."

"Wow! No wonder some of the old dears looked at me a bit old-fashioned!"

"Never mind, Boko; your hat department has raised over three pounds," said Jigger, looking up from his mounting stack of small change. "And Evans and Clarke have raked in even more than that with their gent's natty overcoats and things."

The total grew as one department after another handed in their takings. Some of the amounts were quite small—fifty pence for outdated magazines; seventy-eight pence for gramophone records, and so on. On the other hand the footwear and children's clothing sections both topped the two-pound mark; while the furniture, fire-irons and kitchen knick-knackery returned the handsome sum of five pounds eight pence. This was the largest amount realized by any of the departments; and much of the credit for this was due to the Head-hunter, who had very decently given us an old wardrobe which a dealer had snapped up for two pounds.

We didn't sell everything, of course. There weren't any bids for the bath-chair, and nobody would take the ear-trumpet as a gift! However, Stagg was unlucky over the Doctor's despatch case; it was one of the first articles to be sold.

We crowded round the Treasurer while he added up the last of the takings, and did abstruse calculations in his diary. Finally he said: "This is how we stand to date, chaps. Allowing for the losses on our early efforts, and counting in Boko's collection at the cycle track, our Form's contribution has now reached the magnificent total of £24.57½ p."

Hearty cheers greeted the Treasurer's report. We hadn't reached our target, of course, but at any rate things were better than they had been a week earlier.

"Wacko! Well done, chaps!" I cavorted all round the Hobbies hut in a high-spirited war dance; and I was just starting on the second lap when the door opened and Mrs. Pinafore floated into focus on the threshold.

My war dance ceased in mid-stride. . . . Goodness, how stupid of me! My mind had been so occupied with jumble that I hadn't given another thought to the precious pieces of paper in my pocket. The housekeeper's sudden appearance brought me back to reality with a jolt, and I turned to greet her with a welcoming smile.

"I think I know what you've come for," I said. "Dr. Stallybone accidentally left some papers in his despatch case, didn't he?"

"That's right. Wants 'em back at once. Urgent, he says. So he tells me to come along double quick, before they're sold by mistake."

"There's nothing to worry about," I assured her. "Fortunately, I looked inside his case and took the papers out before the sale begain. They're in my coat pocket. I'll get them for you right away."

I turned to take down my jacket from the wall . . . and found myself confronted by an empty peg.

"That's funny. I'm sure I put it here." I shot an agonized glance at the adjoining pegs, and then felt myself going pale with panic. The walls were bare. My jacket was nowhere to be seen!

"Petrified paintpots! Whatever's happened!" I gasped. Then I called for silence and said: "Listen, chaps. This is important! Has anyone moved a grey jacket from this peg on the wall?"

"Yes, I did," piped up Alfie Cutforth.

I heaved a sigh of relief. Thank goodness for that. Where did you put it?"

"I didn't put it anywhere. I sold it!"

"What!" The room swam before my eyes. "You—you *sold* it?"

"Well, of course. I got thirty p for it. Didn't I do right?"

I thumped the Treasurer's table in exasperation. "You great addle-pated, beetle-headed problem child, Cutforth!" I stormed. "Do you know what you've done? You've gone and sold *my* jacket!"

"Sorry," he mumbled.

"It wasn't meant to be in the sale at all. And what makes it worse is that it's got some private and confidential papers in the pocket."

"Well, how was I to know?" Alfie squawked in defence. "It was next to all the other old clothes, see, so naturally I thought . . ."

"Never mind what you thought. We've got to get the thing back before it falls into the wrong hands. Why, if a foreign agent knew what was in that jacket he'd—he'd—well, goodness knows what *would* happen!"

An odd look spread over Alfie's features. "Foreign agent?" he echoed. "It's funny you should say that."

"Why?"

"Because it was a foreigner I sold it to. Little dark

chap, he was, with an aspidistra and a frying-pan . . . And he wanted that jacket so badly, he wouldn't even wait to see whether it fitted him or not!"

DISAPPEARING TRICK

I STOOD staring at Alfie with dawning horror, my mind in a whirl of speculation. Could the little dark man *really* be in the pay of a foreign power? Was it possible that he had known about the formula all along, and had come to the sale for the express purpose of buying it?

It was an alarming thought; and visions of what might happen next floated before my mind's eye like a serial in a comic strip. I could picture the little man being rushed to a secret airfield where a plane stood ready to smuggle him out of the country. Streaking after him in a high-powered car would be a square-jawed, top-ranking British agent and his youthful assistant, who would reach the airfield in the nick of time. In a series of mental pictures I could follow the desperate gunfight to prevent the plane from taking off. I could see the words "Crack! crack!" issuing in black type from the smoking barrels of their revolvers, and read the snatches of dialogue floating in little balloons above the heads of the characters. ("Ach! So you would attempt to foil my plans. . . . Take that, you meddling fool." . . . *Wham!!*).

At that point my strip cartoon faded out and I came down to earth with a jolt. It was out of the question that the little man could have known the whereabouts of the formula, for no one, apart from Jigger, had seen me transfer the papers before the sale began. Besides, it would have been the despatch case, and not my jacket, that a genuine foreign agent would want to get in his clutches.

But that didn't alter the fact that the little man had the formula in his possession. Who could tell what use he might make of it when he discovered the real value of his bargain? Something would have to be done!

"We must organize a search party at once," I decided. "We've got to get my jacket back, whatever the cost. If we can't trace the chap who bought it, we'll have to go to the police."

"The police?" echoed Boko in amazement. "That's going a bit far, isn't it? I can understand you feeling a bit fed up about losing your coat, but surely it isn't all that important?"

"It jolly well is. Do you know what's inside it? There's a—"

"Ssh!" said Jigger warningly.

I took the hint and *ssh*-ed as per request. Jigger was quite right. The formula was a top priority secret, and the fewer people who knew about it the better.

Mrs. Pinafore had grown fidgety at the mention of the police. "I shouldn't bring them into it—not without Dr. Stallybone's permission, anyway," she said, when I explained that we were unable to give her the papers she'd come for. "If the doctor wants the police he'll call them himself. You'd better leave all that side of it to him."

"Very well, then. Meanwhile we'll do our best to get the papers back for him," I assured her. "I'm terribly sorry this has happened."

She accepted my apology with a disapproving sniff. "So I should think," she said. "Some people are that careless they'd lose their heads if they weren't screwed on properly."

Jigger and I held a short conference after Mrs. Pinafore's departure. We realized it was impossible to enrol volunteers for a search party if we couldn't explain to them what they were supposed to be looking *for*. That meant we should have to do the job ourselves.

"It may not be too difficult," Jigger remarked a few minutes later as we retrieved our raincoats from the cloakroom and set out on our quest "Most of the 'local' foreigners live in the Charlesworth Road district, so I vote we start our inquiries in that direction."

We searched for a couple of hours, calling at all the likely-looking houses advertising Apartments or Bed and Breakfast. The trouble was we didn't know the name of the man we were looking for; and once or twice we received curt answers when we knocked at front doors to ask whether a little blue-chinned chap with an aspidistra and a frying-pan dwelt within. It seemed a hopeless task, but we plodded on with growing despair.

And then, in a dingy boarding-house off Charlesworth Road, wc found the information we were seeking.

"Yerse! I know the gentleman you want. You mean Mr. Pavlowski," said the landlady who answered the door. She was a chatty soul and only too ready to talk about her lodger. "Been living here for over six weeks now, he has. He used to have a job at the electrical factory on the arterial road, only he's given it up lately."

"Oh, I see! May we see him, please?" I asked.

The chatty soul shook her head. "He's not in at the moment. Came back half an hour ago with a lot of rubbish he'd picked up somewhere, and then went straight out again."

"When will he be back?"

The landlady pursed her lips and spread her hands in a gesture of uncertainty. "It's hard to say. He goes off somewhere with his foreign friends on Saturday evenings. Doesn't get back till after midnight as a rule. I'll tell him you called, though."

There was nothing for it but to suspend operations for the time being, and try again when Mr. Pavlowski had returned to his lodgings.

This we did. But when we took up the chase again next day we were too late. . . . The bird had flown.

"Yerse! Packed his bags late last night and cleared off, he did," the landlady told us with gloomy relish when we called at the boarding-house early on the Sunday morning. "Wouldn't say where he was going, either! Soon as I told him two young chaps had been round here asking for him he came over all queer."

"Queer? Queerer than usual, you mean?"

"Oh, yerse. He got the heeby-jeebies something chronic. Said he'd have to clear out while he had the chance. At least, I *think* that's what he said, but his English isn't all that easy to understand."

Our spirits sank to rock-bottom zero: the news couldn't have been worse. Now, everything pointed to the fact that this Pavlowski character had found the formula and was planning to make good use of it. Perhaps the highly-coloured comic strip of my imagination hadn't been so wide of the mark after all!

It was a thousand pities that the landlady had told him of our visit the previous evening, for it was this that must have put him on his guard. After all, he wasn't to know that the "two young chaps" were thirteen-year-old Grammar School boys, and not square-jawed British Secret Service Agents.

There was nothing more we could do, except report our failure to Dr. Stallybone; and with this in mind we thanked the landlady for her trouble and hurried along to the nearest phone box to put a call through to the doctor's house.

The housekeeper answered the phone. She had a bit of a job to fathom what I was saying because her entire tribe of household pets were barking at full volume in the background. . . . *Who* did I say was speaking? she asked me three times . . . Pelican? . . . Billy-an? . . . Oh, *Milligan*! Yes, of course, the jumble sale; she remembered me then! . . . Speak to the doctor? She was sorry, but Dr. Stallybone was out . . . Yes, she'd told him we'd lost the papers, and he'd said we weren't to go to the police. Quite definite he'd been on that point. He was going to deal with the matter himself, and we were to leave everything in his hands. . . .

Frankly, I was surprised that the doctor should take the matter so calmly. I should have thought that the loss of the formula would have put him in no end of a dither and sent him up the wall with worry. It certainly had *me* worried! After all, it was partly my fault that the wretched piece of paper had gone astray, and I'd have done anything to get it back.

"We've done all we can," Jigger consoled me when I'd rung off and relayed the news. "Dr. Stallybone's in charge of this caper and I suppose he knows what he's doing. We'll have to leave it to him and see what happens."

Nothing *did* happen for a week; or rather, nothing happened about the formula. Life didn't exactly standstill, of course, because it was during that week that we agreed to have a return battle with the Tech.

The enemy delivered the challenge just after school dinner on the Thursday. Jigger and I had volunteered to push the roller over a bumpy patch on the Colts XV rugger pitch; and we'd just reached the shed behind the pavilion where the wheelbarrows and tools are kept, when we caught sight of a familiar figure coming across the games field towards us.

"Look who's here!" Jigger exclaimed in surprise. "The one-and-only Spikey Andrews, in person. . . . Hey, Spikey! What are you doing out on the loose at this time of day? I thought you had dinner at school."

Spikey shambled alongside and favoured us with his usual broad grin.

"Some weeks I do—some weeks I don't," he said airily. "I've just been home to my dinner, so I thought I'd stroll back this way and see how all you prehistoric specimens are bearing up." His eye ranged over the garden tools stacked in the shed behind us. "Tut, tut, tut! I'm sorry for you chaps having to make do with that rotten old kit. Now up at the Tech we've got the biggest motor mower in North London. And what's more—"

"Maybe you have, but we don't want to hear about it," I butted in firmly. Spikey needs to be kept in his place, or there's no holding the chap. "And another thing—you're trespassing on Grammar School property. You'll find yourself up no end of a gum tree if one of our masters finds you in our grounds."

Spikey's grin stretched even wider. "They've got to catch me first," he boasted. "I go where I like, see!"

In spite of his easy assurance, I noticed that he was keeping one eye on his line of retreat. He'd obviously found his way in from the lane which runs behind the games field, which explained why he hadn't been seen by any of our masters or prefects.

"What do you want, anyway?" Jigger demanded.

"I just looked in to tell you chaps what a feeble bunch of weak-kneed clodpolls you've got at this school," he informed us in matter-of-fact tones. "Ever since you were lucky enough to get your flag back at the beginning of the term, you haven't had the gumption to challenge us to another battle."

There was some truth in this. "We've been busy raising money for our Great Hall," I reminded him. "If it hadn't been for that we'd have fixed up a return battle weeks ago."

Spikey's grin turned to a sneer. "A good excuse," he said with heavy sarcasm. "Of course, if you're scared to challenge us . . ."

Scared! We weren't going to stand that sort of nonsense from Andrews.

Jigger goggled with indignation. "Don't talk such dehydrated eyewash, Spikey. We'll take you on any time you like—*and* knock you into the middle of next week into the bargain," he said heatedly.

"That sounds more like it," Spikey nodded approvingly. "What about next Saturday, then? Usual time and place, eh?"

"We'll be there," I said. "And this time there won't be any . . . oh, wait a minute, though . . ."

I stopped abruptly because I'd just remembered that our first XV would be playing at home on the Saturday; and we've got a tradition at Sheldrake's that the whole school turns up to watch first XV matches whether they feel like it or not.

The Head-hunter's views on this subject are pretty rigid. He always sets a good example himself by being one of the first to toe the touchline, and he takes jolly good care to see that all the rest of the spectators roll up in time for the kick-off. He won't take excuses, either; and if some slow-moving slacker doesn't arrive on schedule, the H.M. gets the unfortunate specimen in his gun-sights and takes off for a roof-level attack. This is something to be avoided, believe me!

"Let's start at half-past one, Spikey," I suggested. "That'll just give us nice time to put your Technical mob to the slaughter without making us late for our match."

"Fair enough," Spikey agreed. "Only don't be too sure of getting *us* on the run. More likely we shall have to wheel *you* quivering wrecks back to school in your own soap-boxes!"

He grinned again and set off on his return journey across the games field, keeping both eyes on the swivel for stray masters or prefects.

During break next morning Jigger and I enlisted volunteers for the battle. There was no shortage of man-power as all our Fourth form regulars felt it was high time we had another skirmish. On the other hand, there *was* a shortage of vehicles sound in wheel and axle. Our rolling stock had taken some pretty nasty knocks during the last encounter, and one of our self-propelled perambulators was suffering from such a chronic attack of wheel-wobble that we'd had to write it off as a dead loss.

"I just don't know how we're going to replace it," Jigger mused gloomily as we went into class after break. "It's all very well for the Tech—they've probably spent the last few weeks tuning their vehicles up to concert pitch. But we've had our hands so full of jumble sales and whatnot that we haven't had a moment to spare."

At the mention of the jumble sale something went

click inside the brain of R. Milligan, and a bright idea was switched on.

"I've got it!" I exclaimed in triumph. "Why not let's use that old bath-chair that was left over from the sale? It's a trifle rickety on its springs, of course, but it'll travel all right—well *down*hill, anyway!"

"Good scheme," Jigger agreed. "And while you're about it, you might as well take the ear-trumpet along, too. It'd make quite a decent bugle for rallying the troops."

"Wouldn't *you* rather do the bugle calls? After all, you're in charge of the attack," I pointed out.

"No fear," Jigger grinned. "The sight of you charging into action in a bath-chair and brandishing an ear-trumpet will be enough to shake old Spikey's troops rigid. They'll probably rush panic-stricken from the battlefield yelling blue murder!"

THE BATH-CHAIR BATTLE

SHORTLY after quarter-past one the following day, the Sheldrake forces foregathered on the waste ground behind the gasworks. We were all seething with impatience to get to grips with ye foe; and as soon as we'd wheeled our wobbling weapons to action stations Jigger gave us a quick briefing.

"All unmounted chaps will go with Boko Phipps," he ordered. "Dig yourselves in on the slope, and stand by to follow up the main attack after the break-through. The tanks will go into action as soon as the supporting infantry are in position. All clear, Boko?"

"Message received and understood," replied Boko. "Think they'll be using any secret weapons?"

Jigger borrowed Alfie Cutforth's field-glasses and studied the opposite rim of the slope, a hundred yards away, where the Tech Brigade were getting ready for the fray.

"They've got everything pretty well hidden behind their old shed at the moment," Jigger said as he put down the glasses. "Still, if they try any funny business it's up to you infantry chaps to deal with it. We shall have our work cut out getting these tanks up the slope."

"Leave it to us," nodded Boko. "I haven't forgotten the time when Spikey nearly drowned us with that stirrup pump. I'm not taking a chance on *that* happening again!" So saying, the infantry commander opened out a vast moth-eaten umbrella and marched off to battle at the head of his troops.

Then the church clock struck the half hour. . . . We were at war!

Jigger was leading the first assault in his pram—sorry, *tank* I should say—and he'd left me in reserve with the bath-chair. So after giving our chaps a hefty shove-off down the slope, I had time to take a look at the far side of the waste ground which, by this time, was alive with Technical characters slithering into the attack in their armoured vehicles.

At once, I spotted something out of the ordinary. Instead of the usual array of wheeled soap-boxes and captive football bladders, Spikey had collected his equipment from every garden tool shed for miles around—or so it seemed!

There were four wheelbarrows, each with a perspiring navigator on the handles and a bomb-aimer crouching between the shallow sides: there was a wheeled watering-can, the size of a dustbin, and a lawn-mower with a battering ram sticking out in front. Everywhere you looked you could see rakes, brooms, sieves and hose-reels converted into makeshift weapons.

It was more like an allotment holders' meeting than an armoured column on the move, and it pretty soon became clear to me that Spikey's collection of guided missiles was going to come unstuck in no uncertain manner. To start with, the mower sank blade-deep into the soft earth and had to be abandoned. Then, half-way down the slope, the chaps on the barrow handles found they hadn't a hope of keeping things under control, with the gradient against them. The upshot was that the barrows cannoned into one another: two of them overturned and slid upside down to the bottom of the crater, trailing their crews behind them.

It was just about this time that Jigger and his assault party came hurtling down the opposite bank, bumping and bouncing over the uneven ground, and gaining speed every second until . . . *Whomp!* . . . The first soap-box collided heavily with an overturned wheel-barrow, throwing the driver into the scrum of Technical barrow-boys struggling to sort themselves out and regain their feet.

Then Jigger's pram arrived to add to the smash-up, and the whole crater became a heaving mass of revolving wheels and bursting paper bags. To say that the situation was confused would be putting it mildly. Anyway, now that the armoured columns had been knocked for six, Boko decided that it was his turn to start moving.

"Come on, you chaps," he shouted to his infantry. "All out of your foxholes and follow me up the bank. We've got 'em cold, if we go in right away!"

And so it seemed. The enemy's infantry had been

thrown out of gear by the hoo-hah going on all around them, and Boko's men mopped them up left, right and centre. In fact they were half-way up the farther slope and going like blinko, when Spikey turned the tables by producing his famous secret weapon.

He suddenly flitted into focus on the ridge in front of his camp with a garden roller in tow. Then he yelled: "Stand clear, down below!" and sent the thing lolloping over the edge and down the slope, right in the path of Boko and his infantry.

"Look out-jump for it!" yelled Bobo . . . And needless to say, they jumped.

But that wasn't all. From where I stood on top of our bank I could see that the wretched roller was clanking full-tilt towards Jigger Johnson in the crater. And Jig, kneeling down to repair his pram, hadn't a clue that something pretty lethal was going to cannon into the small of his back before the afternoon was fifteen seconds older.

"Jigger!" I yelled. "Look out, man—behind you!"

But he couldn't hear; and no wonder with all that racket going on.

There was only one thing for it. I took a bearing towards Jigger with the front wheel of the bath-chair. Then I gave the thing a mighty shove and scrambled aboard as it hurtled down the slope, leaping the bumps like an ageing kangaroo, and creaking and groaning as loudly as a haunted house. . . . I didn't like to think what would happen if that roller reached the bottom of the crater before I did!

"Hey—Jigger!" I shouted again. . . . And almost before he had time to look up, my ancient chariot was skidding past him and I was dragging him aboard in a sort of neck-high rugger tackle.

At the same moment I jerked the steering-rod hard

over—and cleared the roller by the width of a postage stamp. It rattled past us, smashing the pram to splinters, and leaving a nasty dent in the ground where Jigger had been kneeling less than two seconds before.

"All right, Jig?" I panted.

But he didn't have a chance to answer, because our trusty bath-chair chose that particular moment to turn turtle; after all, it wasn't built for fancy cornering on one wheel. As it landed upside down, the wheels broke aff the chassis and went spinning away, leaving Jigger and me sitting in a cosy little nest of wickerwork and rusty iron springs.

Well, all that rather put a damper on the course of the battle. The fighting came to a sudden stop all over the arena: everybody foregathered in the crater and Spikey found himself facing a spot of terse criticism.

"You dangerous maniac, Andrews," stormed Boko. "You might have killed us! Of all the crazy lunatics I ever met, I reckon you take the first prize for gibbering lunacy. Why can't you stick to the rules?"

Spikey knew that he'd overstepped the mark, but he'll never admit he's in the wrong, whatever happens.

"I told you to watch out," he said, sulkily. "Anyway, if you don't like my way of doing things we'll call the whole thing off." He turned to his supporters. "Come on, chaps; let's get going."

"Just a minute, Spikey," I called as the Tech Brigade began to follow their leader off the battlefield. "What about all these garden tools? Aren't you going to take them with you?"

Spikey turned towards me, and once more the old slow grin spread over his face.

"They're not our tools—they're *yours*," he said. "We 'borrowed' them from the Grammar School tool shed about half an hour ago."

"What!"

Gasps of horror rose from our ranks.

"Yes; I worked it all out last Thursday when I found that back entrance into your playing field," Spikey went on. "Seemed a pity not to make use of it, so we popped in on our way here and helped ourselves to the implements. . . . If I were you, I'd get them back before your headmaster hears about it. He might put the blame on you!"

And away marched Spikey, grinning wider than ever. At his heels trotted the Tech personnel beaming with pride and pleasure at their leader's brilliant strategy.

For some seconds after their departure we stood and stared at one another in dismay.

"Wow! This is going to bish things up properly," moaned Jigger. "The Head will be as livid as two coots if he finds out we've had a battle with the Tech."

We didn't need to be reminded about *that*! The Head-hunter's always talking about the way be ought to behave out of school, and it was obvious that if he got wind of our little skirmish, he'd start creating in no uncertain manner.

"Perhaps we could fox the tools back to the shed without his knowing," suggested Boko.

I glanced at my watch. "We'd better look lively, then. He's going up to school this afternoon to watch the match; and, according to schedule, he's due to stonk past the tool shed in exactly ten minutes from now."

The crux of the crisis was the Head-hunter's well-known habit of punctuality. If we could get to school before he arrived, all might yet be well. If, on the other hand, he should beat us to it, he'd be certain to look askance at our turning up to the match bristling with rakes, spades and watering-cans.

"There's a chance, anyway. We may just do it, if we're lucky," I decided.

We wasted no time. Jigger and I grabbed the roller, Boko took the mower, and the rest of the chaps seized barrows, rakes and what-have-you and lugged them back on to the road. Then the whole clanking circus set off at full-tilt towards the Grammar School.

The Saturday afternoon shoppers in the High Street thought we were stark, raving mad. They gaped at us, pop-eyed with amazement, and then leapt for cover as the wheelbarrows rattled along the pavement, followed by the converted mowing-machine with its blades whirring away at the empty air. Then came the fork-and-spade contingent, with the garden roller rumbling along at the tail-end of the procession.

Panting and exhausted, we staggered back to school and tottered across the quad, *en route* for the tool shed behind the pavilion.

But we didn't quite make it! As we drew level with the flower-beds under the library windows, a car turned in through the school gates and drove across the quad in our direction. A moment later E. C. Hunter, Esq., M.A. (Cantab), was surveying our antics with a jaundiced eye.

"Here it comes! We've had it now," muttered Jigger as the Head stepped out of his car and strolled towards us.

We stood round the flower-beds clutching the tools and feeling extremely foolish. If ever there was a fair cop, this was it!

For a moment the Head-hunter stood looking at our assorted range of garden implements in some bewilderment. Then the expression on his face took a turn for the better and he said: "Well, this is indeed a pleasant surprise. It is most encouraging to see that you boys are willing to come along in good time, and employ the odd half-hour before the match in such a profitable manner."

"I—er—I beg your pardon, sir?" I queried, out of my depth.

He indicated the flower-beds with the point of his shooting-stick. "I have been meaning for some time to have these beds dug over and generally tidied up for the winter. I'm delighted that you should have thought of doing the job without being asked."

We lowered our eyes and studied the toes of our shoes with becoming modesty, while Alfie Cutforth blew his nose to cover his embarrassment—or maybe it was to stifle a nervous giggle. After all, such high praise from the great man was a rare thing in our experience.

"Don't let me disturb the good work," the Head-hunter went on affably. "Carry on until it's time to watch the match."

And off he marched to inspect the pitch, pleased beyond measure at our good deed for the day.

We heaved sighs of relief and set about our task with gusto. Still, it had been a near thing: and it proves what I've always said—you never know where you are with Spikey Andrews!

SPEED TRIAL FOR OLD FAITHFUL

THE first XV were on top of their form that afternoon. Our opponents were the "A" side of a London club—heavier in the scrum than we were, but a shade slower in the line-outs, which evened things up nicely.

Just after the game started, the Frizzer arrived to grace the proceedings with his presence. He parked Old Faithful on the quad, and then joined the Head on the touchline.

"Sorry I'm late, H.M.," he boomed in his cheerful loudhailer of a voice. "I'd have been here twenty minutes ago, only the old bus blew a gasket last week and she's still suffering from shock."

The Head-hunter nodded—a little distantly I thought. Between you and me, I don't think his orderly mind approves of unreliable contraptions like Old Faithful; but of course he didn't say anything as we were all milling around within earshot.

Well, after that we all got down to some full-throated cheering, and yelled encouragement for Sheldrake until we were as hoarse as a bevy of bullfrogs. It was a good game to watch. Both teams tore into the attack as though the fate of an empire was at stake, and neither side could get much of an advantage over the other. The score was six-all when the final whistle blew, and most chaps agreed that the drawn game was a pretty fair indication of the afternoon's play.

Mr. Frisby overtook Jigger and me as we were strolling away from the pitch together after the match was over.

"Good game wasn't it, sir?" said Jigger chattily.

"Splendid, splendid!" the Frizzer agreed. A thought struck him and he added: "Are you chaps going my way? I'll give you a lift home if you like."

"Thanks very much, sir," we chorused, trying our best to sound enthusiastic about the treat in store.

As you know there's a catch about accepting lifts in Old Faithful; once you've enrolled as a passenger, you have to work your passage by pushing ye chariot whenever she feels obstinate. Still, it keeps you fit and it's better exercise than walking.

"Jump in, then," quoth the Frizzer. "I daresay you'll be glad of a comfortable seat after standing on the touchline all afternoon, eh?"

"Oh yes, sir—rather, sir. Jolly decent of you to give us a lift, sir." After all, you have to humour these well-meaning adults occasionally, or they begin to think they're not being appreciated.

So we climbed aboard, ready to bale out and push at a moment's notice; but oddly enough this wasn't necessary. At the eighth pull on the starter the engine coughed like an asthmatic sea-lion and spluttered into action. Old Faithful's body-work quivered like a jelly in a railway restaurant car, and we chugged out of the school gates at an unsteady twelve m.p.h.

It was beginning to grow dark by now, though the shops were still open and crowded with late-afternoon customers. Saturday is always a busy day in our High Street, and round about tea-time the pavements are wedged solid with hordes of citizens whom you never seem to meet at any other time of the week.

All went well for a quarter of a mile. Then, just as we were coming up to a zebra crossing, an optimistic pedestrian stepped off the pavement in front of us, and headed across the road. He was well within his rights, of course: the only thing he didn't allow for was the fact that Old Faithful takes umbrage if she's pulled up too suddenly.

The Frizzer did his best to cope with the crisis. He jammed on the brakes so hard that Old Faithful rocked on her chassis like a dinghy in a gale. As the brakes screeched on, the car skidded forward with locked wheels and shuddering shock-absorbers, and came to a stop on the studs of the crossing. A fountain of boiling water shot out of the ill-fitting radiator cap, drenching the bonnet and windscreen in a torrential downpour. The front springs twanged like harp-strings; the back axle groaned in anguish; the engine stalled. . . .

"Tut-tut-tut!" said Mr. Frisby.

The unwary walker had leaped like a mountain goat at the first shrill squawk of the brakes. As he came down to ground level, he shot a nervous glance in our direction before bolting for safety to the opposite pavement.

I gripped Jigger by the arm. "See who it is?" I gasped in surprise.

Jigger stared hard at the fleeing pedestrian. "It's nobody I know," he said blankly. Then I remembered that he had never seen our foreign friend at close quarters.

"It's Mr. Pavlowski—the chap who snaffled the formula!" I shouted excitedly.

"Gosh! Are you sure?"

"Of course I'm sure. Dash it all, I ought to know. Besides, he's still wearing my jacket!"

Jigger flung open the off-side door of the car. "Come on then, Rex—what are you waiting for? Let's catch him before he disappears."

We jumped down on to the road. Mr. Frisby must have thought we were disembarking to give Old Faithful the usual push, because he called out: "Hang on a minute, chaps. I'll try the starter first."

"Sorry, sir, we can't wait," I said in urgent tones. "I hope you don't mind if we go on ahead, but we're in a supersonic hurry, sir."

It wasn't, perhaps, the most tactful way of putting it, because no proud motorist likes being reminded that a rheumaticky tortoise could knock spots off his car in a speed trial. What I really meant—if only I could have stopped to explain—was that, as the man we were chasing was now threading his way in and out of the crowd, it would be easier for us to catch him up on foot.

Anyway, we dashed across the road, hot foot in pursuit, leaving Mr. Frisby stroking his moustache in perplexity and wondering what the modern generation of teen-agers was coming to.

Mr. Pavlowski was only a few yards ahead when we reached the further pavement. We quickened our pace until we caught up with him. Then I tapped him on the shoulder.

"Excuse me, I'd like a word with you," I began.

I got no further! He gave one guilty gulp and shot off into the crowd like a startled rabbit.

"After him, quick," said Jigger; and away we went, weaving in and out of the jostling crowd in a desperate effort to keep our quarry in sight.

Mr. Pavlowski tried every trick he could think of to throw off the pursuit. After battling against the crowd for fifty yards he suddenly dived into Woolworth's, hoping that we hadn't seen him, and would go hurrying past.

But the ruse didn't work. "There he goes!" cried Jigger. "I caught sight of your jacket disappearing through the swing door."

The store was packed from end to end with customers. At first we couldn't see our quarry anywhere; but after traipsing round the stationery department and nearly getting marooned amongst the ladies' overalls, I caught a glimpse of the little man amongst the electrical equipment on the far side of the store.

"We'll never catch up with him in here," moaned Jigger. "He's only got to make his way round with the crowd and he'll be back in the street again before we can get near him."

"We'll split up," I decided. "You follow him from behind, while I make my way round in a circle and bear down on him from the opposite direction."

We ploughed our separate ways into the crowd, and for some minutes I lost sight of both Jigger and Mr. Pavlowski. I began to grow anxious. Our suspected foreign agent must be caught at all costs. His wild dash for freedom confirmed my fears that he was in the espionage business up to his eyebrows. Whatever happened, we mustn't let him slip through our fingers this time!

I edged my way past the fancy jewellery, skirted the men's socks and came out by the biscuit counter at the far end of the building. According to my theory, Mr. Pavlowski should now be making his way towards me. My gaze roamed the crowd. . . . Yes, there he was, about fifteen feet away and heading in my direction.

Near at hand were two large ladies discussing the price of cheese, so I took cover behind them and made a further quick reconnaissance. Yes, there was old Jigger following hard on the heels of the quarry. Mr. Pavlowski was nicely sandwiched between the two of us. This was the moment to pounce!

I stepped out from behind my screen of large ladies, and moved forward to bar the little man's progress. He spotted me at once, and wheeled round retrace his steps—and then he saw Jigger coming up behind him.

For a second Mr. Pavlowski hesitated. Then he darted sideways through a gap between two counters. Ahead of him was an emergency exit which I hadn't noticed until that moment. He hurled himself at the double doors which swung open as he pushed the iron bar holding them in position. The next second he was outside the building, and heading back towards the High Street as fast as his crepe soles would carry him.

Jigger and I were after him in a flash, but he'd got a few yards start. As we regained the High Street, Mr. Pavlowski left the pavement and dashed into the midst of the traffic without a thought for the rules of the Highway Code. He side-stepped a taxi, dodged round a lorry and then raced for a bus which was just drawing up at a request stop.

We followed as fast as we could, keeping an eye on the traffic and doing a brisk kerb drill at the same time. As luck would have it, we had to wait for a couple of motor-bikes to go past, and by the time we panted up to the request stop the bus was thirty yards away—with Mr. Pavlowski aboard, of course.

I always think that these awkward situations are handled much better on television than ever they are in real life. You know the sort of thing I mean. When the villain makes a getaway in a fast car there's always another one cruising along just behind. So all the hero has to do is to leap aboard, shouting: "Follow that car in front—and step on it!" And away they go, with no questions asked.

But things didn't work out so smoothly for Jigger and me. The only thing coming along behind was a London Transport bus, and you can't leap on to buses and order the conductor to follow the double-decker in front. Well, you *could*, of course, but we should have got an old-fashioned look if we'd tried it because each vehicle was heading for a different destination.

Still, we did our best. "Hop on quick, Jig," I ordered as the bus drew up at the stop. "We may be able to catch him before his bus turns off the High Street."

"Pass right down inside," said the conductor briskly as we jumped on to the platform.

"Couldn't we stay here?" I pleaded. "We may want to get off in a hurry and . . ."

"Standing room inside: seats on top."

"But we don't *want* to go on top!"

"Then pass right down inside, and stop blocking the gangway."

Five more passengers came swarming aboard at that moment. They piled up behind us on the platform and we found ourselves swept into the lower deck by sheer weight of numbers.

"This is frantic," groaned Jigger as we came to rest hard up against the front window. "We shan't have a hope of nipping off quickly!"

"Never mind. At least we can keep tabs on the bus in front."

Our conductor jerked the bell rope and we set off at a lively pace. We hadn't gone far before we caught sight of the other bus ahead, which had come to rest at a traffic light.

"Good-o! We're catching it up," I crowed. "I vote we try and change buses at the next . . ."

I broke off in dismay. The traffic lights had changed to green; and as the bus ahead moved forward so Mr. Pavlowski stepped on to the pavement, and set off down a side road at a trot.

"Wow! Let's get off quick," I gasped. "He's giving us the slip."

We struggled back along the bus, which was now travelling at top speed in order to pass the lights while they were still in its favour. We weren't popular with the passengers who'd come in just behind us, even though we did our best not to tread on their chilblains as we squeezed past mumbling apologies.

"Hey! Where d'you think you're going?" the conductor demanded as we arrived panting and breathless on the platform.

"Stop the bus, please. We want to get off!" I said.

"Get off? But you've only just got *on*!"

"Yes, I know. We made a mistake. This is the wrong bus—I mean, it's going the wrong way, or rather . . ."

"Well, you can't get off between stops," the conductor said firmly. "Nice sort of carry-on, I must say. Next time you catch a bus you want to make up your mind whether you're coming or going before you get on."

We left the bus at the next stop and hurried back to the traffic lights. There was no sign of Mr. Pavlowski, of course; and although we knew which direction he'd taken there didn't seem much chance of catching him up, now that he'd had so long a start.

As we stood on the corner trying to decide our next move, the sound of jangling machinery was wafted down the road towards us, and the next moment Old Faithful chugged into focus, with the Frizzer seated proudly at the wheel.

"She's going well to have got this far already," Jigger observed. "D'you think she could catch up with this Pavlowski bird if she puts her back into it?"

"It's worth trying, anyway. If we tell the Frizzer what's been happening, he may be only too keen to lend a hand."

We hopped up and down waving our arms like windmill sails to attract Mr. Frisby's attention. Fortunately he saw us: he pulled in to the kerb and throttled back the mighty motor to a steady note of *a-junka-junka-junka.*

"What on earth are you boys playing at?" he wanted to know.

"Terribly sorry to dash off like that, sir, but I saw someone wearing my coat," I apologized.

The Frizzer raised an inquiring eyebrow, so I went on and told him how Cutforth had sold it by mistake at the jumble sale. I didn't say anything about the formula because there wasn't time to go into details. We'd have to get moving right away if we wanted to see Mr. Pavlowski again.

"So you want to catch this chap up and ask him a few pertinent questions about your jacket, eh?" boomed the Frizzer. "In you get, then. We'll see what can be done."

I'm never going to utter another unkind word about Old Faithful. That car is worth its weight in uranium, and you can quote me as saying so.

No sooner had Mr. Frisby let in the clutch than we roared off down the side road with all four cylinders working overtime, and straining at the leash like nobody's business. Mind you, I'm not saying it was a comfortable trip. The old crock shuddered and shook like a jet aircraft trying to crash the sound barrier; though a glance at the speedometer was enough to dispel any doubt that we were approaching supersonic speed. Still, nineteen m.p.h. isn't bad going when you're chasing a middle-aged man puffing along on foot. And when the speedometer needle crept up to the twenty-two m.p.h. mark, I felt that our quarry was as good as in the bag already.

At least, I *think* we touched twenty-two m.p.h. It was difficult to get the speedometer in clear focus because the whole of the car was shimmering with vibration. So were the occupants! From where I sat the Frizzer looked like a man viewed through a heat haze

—a trifle blurred round the edges, with the points of his vast moustache quivering like aspens.

"Keep it up, sir," I encouraged him.

"Rather!" he boomed back. "Going like a bird, isn't she!"

Mr. Frisby's remark was nearer the truth than he imagined; for at that moment a gust of wind swirled in through the gaping side-screens and lifted the hood from its front moorings. With a sudden *swoosh* the ancient canopy billowed up, held only by its rear stays. For some seconds it flapped and beat the air like an unwieldy kite struggling to become airborne: then it collapsed, folding itself neatly over the heads of the driver and passengers, and reducing visibility to a total black-out.

I'm not quite sure what happened next, because the situation became confused. All I know is, we swerved and hit the near-side kerb with a bump that knocked the spare wheel off its bracket and sent it bouncing down on to the road with a thud.

After that, Old Faithful came to rest broadside across the road, while we three occupants tunnelled our way back to the surface from beneath the flapping envelope of canvas.

"Pity about that," Mr. Frisby remarked as he emerged into the twilight. "And just as we'd got going so well. I was rather hoping for a four-minute mile on this level stretch! Never mind; press on regardless, what!"

Whereupon we all set about getting Old Faithful back on the beam. Jigger and I made fast the hood, while the Frizzer clambered down on to the roadway and replaced the spare wheel. The car's lights had gone out when she struck the kerb. However, a few hearty smacks on the wings joined up the loose connections and restored the illuminations to their usual dim glimmer. . . . Then we started off again.

"I've got a feeling we're wasting our time," Jigger said when we'd covered a few hundred yards without sighting our quarry. "How do we know he's still ahead of us? He could have beetled off down any of these side turnings without our knowing."

"We'll have to chance it," I answered; though by now I was beginning to feel that the quest was pretty hopeless. "Anyway, I vote we carry on to the end of this road, and if we haven't spotted him by then . . . Golly! There he is!"

There was no doubt about it. Thirty yards ahead, the short, squat figure of Mr. Pavlowski was plainly visible in the rays of a street lamp. He wasn't hurrying, either; he was strolling along with the carefree swagger of one who has successfully shaken off his pursuers. I couldn't help smiling. He little knew the shock that was coming to him!

"That's the chap, sir," I said to Frizzer. "Will you pull up beside him, please?"

Mr. Frisby seemed a shade doubtful, now that the time had come to interfere with the liberties of a fellow citizen. After all, England was a free country!

"M'yes; but don't forget, Milligan, that you'll have to ask him tactfully if you want your coat back," he replied as the car slackened speed. "He's not obliged to return it now that he's paid for the thing. Besides, you can hardly expect him to walk home in his shirt-sleeves."

We knew better, of course! And Jigger's voice sounded grim and determined as he muttered. "He's jolly well got to give it back—*and* what he found in the pockets, too! If he turns nasty we'll march him along to the nearest police station."

"Don't talk nonsense, boy," retorted the Frizzer. "The police have got quite enough to do without bothering their heads over slight misunderstandings about who is wearing who's sports jacket. You'll never get this fellow to go to the police station, you mark my words!"

By this time the car had drawn level with the unsuspecting Mr. Pavlowski. As it came to a stop, Jigger and I jumped out and closed in on the little man before he realized what was happening.

"Excuse me! I'd like a word with you," I said politely.

For the space of a second he stared at me in wild alarm, and then glanced quickly about him, seeking a way to escape.

He found none. . . . Left, right and centre he was hemmed in by Jigger, by me, and by Old Faithful at the kerb; while across the pavement behind him three stone steps led only to a gaunt, grey building with small windows and a glass-panelled swing-door.

Panic seized Mr. Pavlowski. Without knowing what he was doing he turned and rushed blindly up the three stone steps, and disappeared through the swing-door before we could lift a finger to stop him.

I wasn't worried, though. You see, I'd just spotted a blue lamp hanging above the entrance. The building was a Police Station.

MR. PAVLOWSKI

It took the sergeant on duty at the enquiry counter a little while to sort out exactly what was going on in his well- ordered police station. And not without reason. . . .

First, Mr. Pavlowski came stampeding through the door in wide-eyed woe, waving his arms like semaphore flags and gabbling at full volume in some unidentified foreign tongue. Hard on his heels came Messrs. J. Johnson and R. Milligan, flushed with the excitement of the chase, and followed, a moment later, by Mr. Frisby, looking a trifle nonplussed at the unexpected turn of events.

"Hey! Steady on, steady on. What's the trouble?" the sergeant demanded, laying down his pen and rising to cope with the unruly invasion.

Now, I'd been expecting Mr. Pavlowski to recoil in horror when he found himself face to face with a policeman. But not a bit of it. He rushed up to the sergeant in joyful relief; I think he'd have embraced him if only he'd been tall enough.

"Pliss, you save me frim diss pipples, yes?" he asked anxiously, flapping a hand in our direction. "Diss pipples are very bad pipples. Dey 'ave try to catnip me, you unnerstan'?"

"They tried to do *what*?" queried the sergeant.

Mr. Pavlowski searched his brain for the right word. "Cadnop . . . codnap . . . kidnap!" be hazarded.

The sergeant looked hard at Mr. Frisby. "*Did* you try to kidnap this man?"

"Eh! Good gracious, no. Dash it all, I mean to say—well, really!" protested the Frizzer in flabbergasted amazement.

"Yes, yes. Dey 'ave try, two times. You arrest me from diss pipples, yes? You take me into your protected custard, no?" urged Mr. Pavlowski.

This had the sergeant worried for a moment, until the Frizzer came to the rescue with an English translation.

"I think he wants to be arrested and taken into protective custody," he explained.

"H'm!" said the sergeant. "We'd better try and find out what it's all in aid of first."

I took a step forward . . . R. Milligan's big moment had arrived!

"I can tell you what it's all about," I announced in ringing tones. "This man's a foreign agent. We've been chasing him because he's managed to get hold of a secret formula belonging to the Atomic Research Commission, and we've been on his tracks ever since."

The sergeant obviously didn't believe me.

"And how did he obtain possession of this closely-guarded document, may I ask?"

"He—er, well, he bought it at a jumble sale, as a matter of fact."

Yes, I know my theory sounded just a *leetle* improbable when spoken aloud. The sergeant thought so, too. He heaved a deep sigh and raised despairing eyes to the ceiling. Only too clearly I could read the thoughts passing through his mind. "Why do I have to waste my time listening to raving lunatics prattling nonsensical balderdash when I've got better things to do!" he seemed to be asking himself.

He didn't say this out loud, of course. But when he deigned to answer me he put on the sort of voice you use when a backward five-year-old tells you he's just seen fairies at the bottom of the garden.

"Well, well, fancy that! So they sell these things at jumble sales, do they?" he said, without a flicker of a smile. "You buy them by the packet, I suppose—or do they come cheaper by the dozen?"

My startling news item didn't seem to be going down very well.

"It's true, anyway," I persisted. "You see, quite by chance it happened to be in the pocket of a jacket he bought; the same jacket he's wearing now."

"Dear me!" said the sergeant, in the same deadpan tone of polite disbelief. He turned to Mr. Pavlowski to hear what he had to say about the fantastic charge levelled against him.

"Dere is nozzing in the pockets when I buy him at the chompell sell," the little man proclaimed. "Nozzing at all, only dirty 'andkerchief and bondle of notpippers. Look I show you!"

He rummaged in the lining of the inside pocket and brought out a sheaf of note-paper which he laid on the sergeant's desk. I craned forward to read the top sheet, and a row of algebrical symbols caught my eye. There was no doubt about it; it was Dr. Stallybone's formula, right enough.

The sergeant's expression changed as he caught sight of the heading. *Atomic Research Commission. . . . Top Secret.* With growing concern he read through the first paragraph.

"Circulation restricted to 'H' Group Research Personnel. For security reasons this memorandum is not to be removed from Admin. Room M/47, or the data divulged to unauthorized persons."

He pored over the remainder of the page for a few moments and then said: "This is growing interesting."

Mr. Pavlowski gave him a beaming smile. "You like it, yes?" he inquired brightly.

"No, I don't like it at all," returned the sergeant shortly. "And to start with, you can tell me what you know about this piece of paper."

"I know nozzing. I 'ave not read him."

"You haven't read it?" echoed the sergeant. "You don't expect me to believe that, do you?"

" 'Ow can I read him when nobody 'as learnt me? I spik English, but I do not read or write him—only a few words."

I thought I could spot a flaw in that argument. "If you didn't know what was on this paper, why did you run away when I spoke to you?" I asked.

"I 'ave not know you want diss pipper. I t'ink you kadnip me so I 'ave to go away from England, no?"

"I don't understand all this. Let's start at the beginning and get this kidnapping business sorted out," said the sergeant.

The little man was only too willing to talk, though he wasn't very easy to follow. In fact, it took the police sergeant about twenty minutes to make head or tail of the story. But at last he pieced it together, helped by the Frizzer as a sort of unofficial interpreter.

It seemed that Mr. Pavlowski had escaped from his own country, and had come to England as a refugee. I never did find out exactly where he came from, but I gathered that the government of his native land took a pretty poor view of people who sought political asylum abroad. That being so, they had agents attached to their embassy in London whose duty it was to round up these straying fellow-countrymen and persuade them to pack their bags and go home. There were ways and means, it seemed, of repatriating obstinate refugees against their will. Whether or not they were willing to go didn't seem to matter; it was a case of doing what they were told—or else!

Anyway, Mr. Pavlowski had seen the red light. The agents had recently been active in the Charlesworth Road district, and he knew for a fact that he would be on the short list when the next bout of repatriation got going in a big way. So, when he'd heard from his landlady the previous Saturday that two unidentified characters had been round making inquiries about him, he decided to change his lodgings and disappear while the going was good.

For a whole week he'd felt confident that he'd covered his tracks. And then, while walking in the High Street half an hour before, he had felt the tap on his shoulder and had heard the dreaded invitation: "Excuse me; I'd like a word with you."

That had been more than enough for Mr. Pavlowski. He had taken to his heels without waiting to find out what his pursuers wanted to see him about. A little quiet reflection would no doubt have told him that thirteen-year-old schoolboys could hardly have been the agents of a foreign government whom he was so anxious to avoid. But Mr. Pavlowski hadn't stopped to reason; and frankly I can't say I blamed him. For all he knew, the whole thing might have been a ruse to catch him off his guard.

One thing, however, was perfectly clear. Dr. Stallybone's formula meant less than nothing to Mr. Pavlowski, whose knowledge of English was so sketchy that he hadn't the foggiest notion of what the fateful sheet of paper was all about.

"I'm sorry I caused you all this trouble," I apologized when the tale was told and the sergeant had checked all the facts. "But you see we just *had* to get that formula back and—well, you did carry on in a rather suspicious manner, didn't you?"

The little man gave me a broad, beaming smile. "Dat's all right. No 'ard fillings? All goot frients togedder, no? And I can kip the goat, yes?"

I hadn't the heart to refuse him. "Yes, you can keep the coat," I said. After all, it was an old one, and my mother had already written it off as a dead loss.

The sergeant was still brooding over the more serious aspect of the little man's story.

"No one can force you to leave this country if you've got permission ta stay here," he said ."I'll look into the business and find out what can be done. In the meantime, you come straight along here and tell me if these chaps try any more hanky-panky, you understand?"

Mr. Pavlowski looked blank. "What, pliss, means honky-pinky?"

The sergeant wasn't prepared for that one. He rubbed his chin thoughtfully and said: "Well, it's what you might call—er—um—jiggery-pokery, if you follow me."

"And what means diss piggery-jokery, pliss?"

This time the sergeant was beaten. He cast a look of appeal at the Frizzer, who did his best to translate.

"It means you're to come here and tell the sergeant if these people try to make you do anything that you don't want to do."

"Yes, yes, I unnerstan'," Mr. Pavlowski nodded earnestly. "No more honky-piggery from diss pipples, or I come 'ere and spill the bins, yes?"

"That's the general idea—more or less," the Frizzer agreed. After which the little man shook hands all round, left his address with the sergeant, and trotted off happily into the night.

Well, the next item on the agenda was to contact Dr. Stallybone and restore his precious documents. With this in mind the sergeant bundled Jigger and me into a police car and drove to the doctor's house.

The Frizzer decided to come along too, and said he would follow up behind in Old Faithful. But unfortunately the old bus found the pace too hot for her. Somewhere along the road she gave up the struggle, and we didn't see Mr. Frisby or his trusty chariot again until we got to school on Monday morning.

It was getting on for seven o'clock when we arrived at Dr. Stallybone's house. So much had happened during the last couple of hours that I had lost count of time; I'd even forgotten that I hadn't had my tea, until the smell of Mrs. Pinafore's cooking came wafting out into the hall, to remind me how hungry I really was.

Dr. Stallybone was delighted to hear that his papers had been found; at the same time, he seemed just a trifle embarrassed at having them returned to him by a policeman.

"You shouldn't have gone to all this trouble," he said as he ushered us into his study. He fussed around for a few moments, removing various dogs from the best armchairs so that he could offer us all a seat. Then he went on: "Of course it was most inconvenient being without my notes, but I hardly liked to approach the police over a trifling matter of this kind."

We stared at him. . . . *Trifling?* Was the man out of his mind? Was the loss of a top secret atomic formula to be looked upon as an everyday occurrence?

"I can quite see you were anxious to avoid publicity," said the sergeant, handing off a couple of poodles which were trying to climb on to his knee. "On the other hand, I can't regard a matter like this as unimportant. Perhaps you'd be good enough to check the papers and make sure they are complete. I didn't read them myself—not beyond the first page, that is, on account of it being marked confidential."

"No; we didn't look at the other pages, either," Jigger chimed in.

Dr. Stallybone took the papers from the sergeant's outstretched hand and peered at them through the lower half of his gold-rimmed bi-focals. He frowned doubtfully at the first page which he put on one side, and then examined the rest of the sheets with growing interest.

"Ah, yes, they all seem to be here, thank you. I am more than grateful to have them back, I can tell you. I had promised the editor of the *Ornithological Review* that I'd send them on to him, and he was growing a little anxious in case they didn't arrive before the magazine went to press."

Once more we goggled at the man in stupefied amazement. Surely he wasn't intending to publish these secret documents for the perusal of all and sundry! Why, it was enough to rock Admin. room M/47 to its foundations, and cause "H" Group research personnel to gibber with horror!

"But isn't it secret?" I gasped.

The doctor's eyebrows rose in surprise. "Good heavens, no! There's nothing secret about an article on the nesting habits of the lesser spotted woodpecker!"

"The lesser spotted *what*!" cried Jigger, aghast.

"Woodpecker," repeated Dr. Stallybone. "The lesser spotted variety is, as you know, easily distinguished from its larger colleague not only by its appearance, but also by its note. It goes *cheek-cheek-cheek* in contrast to the sharp *chack-chack* of the greater spotted woodpecker, which in its turn is very different from the sound of the green woodpecker which can be likened to a loud, echoing laugh—*ha-ha-ha*, or in some cases *hellow-hellow-hellow* . . ."

By this time the doctor was so engrossed in his lecture that I think he would have gone on for the rest of the evening, *ha-ha-ha*-ing and *hellow-hellow-hellow*-ing at full volume—and might even have proceeded to give us a demonstration of practical woodpecking on the door panels. But it was not to be. Interesting though the subject was, this was hardly the moment, we felt, for a discourse on feathered songsters.

The sergeant jumped to his feet with a muffled exclamation and seized the sheaf of papers which were lying on the table. Jigger and I hurried to his side: and for the first time we were able to examine the contents in detail.

We were in for a shock. . . . Apart from the formula on the first page, the rest of the papers consisted of a harmless-looking article on bird-watching! We stared at the typewritten sheets in some perplexity.

"But what about this business on page one?" queried the sergeant at length. "What's a secret document on atomic physics doing all mixed up with your bird-watching notes?"

Dr. Stallybone ran his eye over Section IX of the *ATIR* scheme with scant interest. "I haven't the faintest idea," he murmured. "I've never seen this document before in my life."

"But it was in your despatch case along with these other papers," Jigger pointed out.

"Really! I wonder how it got there." Dr. Stallybone scratched his nose thoughtfully as he studied the algebraical symbols. "I'm afraid I don't understand this at all. Perhaps you can enlighten me?"

"Surely you can follow the formula," I said, "You're an expert on atomic physics and all that sort of stuff, aren't you?"

"Me? Good gracious, no! I have no knowledge of the subject whatsoever. My own scientific researches have been confined exclusively to the study of bird life in all its phases."

As though in confirmation of this statement, the doctor waved his hand at the bookshelves lining the wall behind him. Row upon row of books met my gaze: and I noticed that one whole shelf was devoted to learned-looking tomes about various fowls of the air. In each case the author was Arthur J. Stallybone, M.A., D.Sc., F.Z.S.

I could have kicked myself for leaping to hasty conclusions. It was that prize clodpoll, J. C. Stagg, who had first sown the idea in my mind that Dr. Stallybone was a nuclear physicist, and, like an idiot, I hadn't bothered to check the facts. That's what came of reading comic strips, where *all* scientists turn out to be atomic experts who spend their time inventing bigger and better flying saucers.

There was a painful silence after the doctor had spoken. Then the sergeant gave us a reproachful look and said: "We seem to be barking up the wrong tree." He picked up the formula and put it in his pocket. "I think I'd better take care of this, Doctor. And now, if you'll excuse me, I'll get back to the station and make a few more inquiries."

"Anything we can do to help, Sergeant?" I asked eagerly.

He shook his head. "Much obliged for the offer, but I reckon I'll get on a lot quicker by myself," he said in flat, deadpan tones of mild sarcasm. "Mind you, I'm grateful for what you lads have done . . ."

"Thanks very much," we beamed, flattered by this high praise.

"Don't mention it. Very helpful you've been, the pair of you. First your foreign agent turns out to be a harmless refugee, and now your atomic scientist tells me he's a lesser-spotted bird-watcher."

He turned in the doorway and delivered his parting shot. "If we go on like this much longer, we'll probably find that the secret formula is a recipe for somebody's perishing plum pudding!"

STAGGERS SETS THE ALARM

For some minutes after the sergeant had left, my mind was in a daze of confusion. Who had hidden the formula in the doctor's despatch case? How had it been smuggled out of Admin. Room M/47, under the very noses of "H" Group Research personnel? Dr. Stallybone didn't know; neither did we. Even the trained brain of our long-suffering sergeant could provide no ready solution—in spite of all our help!

I'm afraid the sergeant took rather a jaundiced view of our part in the proceedings. He seemed to think that we'd led him on a wild goose chase, and up to a point he was right. But, I ask you, was it *our* fault?

Dr. Stallybone, on the other hand, was more than friendly. Atomic formulae meant less than nothing to one of his quiet tastes, though birds and bird-watching meant a great deal. And he was so overjoyed at having his manuscript returned in good order that he wanted to give us a cheque for a pound as a contribution to the Great Hall Repair Fund. But unfortunately, he couldn't find his cheque-book amongst the untidy litter on his roll-top desk.

"It's most annoying. I know I left it here somewhere," he murmured, rummaging vaguely through the pigeon-holes. After ten minutes' vain search he gave it up and said: "I won't detain you any longer now. Perhaps it would be convenient if I came along to your school on Monday morning and made my little donation then?"

"Yes, I'm sure that would be all right," I told him. "I'll tell the Head that you're coming, shall I?"

"Please do. I shall be delighted to meet him."

As it happened, I forgot all about the message as soon as I arrived home, because my one-track mind was still absorbed with the question of the formula. I couldn't see daylight, whichever way I looked at it, and by Sunday evening I'd come to the conclusion that the whole baffling business must rank as one of the unsolved mysteries of modern times.

I was still brooding over the matter as I pedalled along to school on Monday morning. However, when I arrived at ye ancient seat of learning I had to switch my train of thought on to a siding, because Alfie Cutforth pranced up and buttonholed me, almost before I'd got my nose inside the gate.

"I say, Milligan, what do you think?" he began in an excited latest-news-bulletin tone of voice. "I've been doing a spot of secret service work over the week-end and I've unearthed a plot. Would you like to hear about it?"

I'd heard some of Alfie's sensational discoveries in the past and I was in no mood to waste time listening to another one. So I said: "Not just now, if you don't mind. Some other time, perhaps. At the moment I'm trying to . . ."

"Well, I'll tell you, then," Alfie went on, falling into step beside me as I wheeled my machine across the quad to the bike shed. "It's about Spikey Andrews. He was swanking like blinko before the battle on Saturday—telling all his mob just how he was going to collar our flag. And then, of course, he bished up the issue with that crazy garden roller stunt, and it didn't come off. Ever so fed up, he was, according to what I heard."

So many things had happened since the bathchair battle that I'd almost forgotten the Tech Brigade and all their wondrous works.

"I can't help Spikey's troubles. I've got enough of my own," I answered. But Alfie was bursting to tell me more so I gave in and said: "Go on, then. What is this famous plot, anyway?"

"Well, I happened to meet Bubblegum on the borough rec. yesterday," Alfie went on. "And quite by accident he let out that they've got a secret surprise planned for us. He wouldn't say what it was, of course, but putting two and two together I gather that Spikey's going to try and fox into our premises some time today when we're not expecting it."

"I wouldn't put it past him. He did the same thing only last week. But what's the big idea when he gets here?"

"Well, if you ask me, there's only one thing he *could* want—and that's our flag. You see, if he filched it from right inside the enemy stronghold, he'd be able to strut round the Tech with his thumbs in his armpits for the rest of the term. There'd be no holding the chap with a thing like that to swank about."

Now, A. Cutforth is a bit of a scaremonger, as I think I've told you before, but it seemed to me that this time the boy was bang on the target.

To start with, Spikey hadn't forgiven me for salvaging our banner from the Tech bicycle shed at the beginning of the term. Furthermore, it was common knowledge that Jigger kept the trophy in his locker in the corridor outside Form 4 classroom. What could be simpler, therefore, than for Spikey to slip into Sheldrake's *via* the back entrance? If he chose the right moment and planned the operation with some care, he could whip the flag out of the locker marked J. I. G. Johnson, and then charge hot-hoof away from the scene of the crime without anyone knowing he'd been on the premises at all.

"This is serious! We shall have to do something about it," I said, coming to a sudden stop. "Of course, we could easily hide the flag somewhere else today, but . . ."

"Don't talk such feeble-minded eyewash!" Alfie broke in impatiently. "We don't want *only* to stop him finding the thing. We want to catch him red-handed and make it so hot for the poor misguided clodpoll that he'll never try the same dodge again."

"Yes, but how? I foresee snags. Of course, if he comes during the lunch break we can keep watch, but I don't quite see . . ."

"He won't come during the lunch break. He'll come while we're all in school."

"Talk sense! He'll be in school himself, won't he?"

A satisfied smirk spread slowly over the Cutforth countenance, and he prodded a grimy forefinger at me to emphasize the importance of his remarks.

"Ah! That's where my superior powers of deduction come in. There's a Borough Council by-election today, and they're using the Tech as one of the polling stations."

This was perfectly true. From time to time, the Tech and most of the primary schools were lucky enough to bag an extra day's holiday when their buildings were commandeered by the authorities for local government elections. It was a sore point with us that they never used the Grammar School for this purpose, though we'd have been more than willing to sacrifice our studies in such a worthy cause.

"He's bound to make the attempt today, because it's the only time that he'll be out on the loose while we're cooped up in the classroom," Alfie argued. "But you needn't get in a flap, because I've got everything nicely organized. The Staggers and I spent all yesterday afternoon perfecting our plans: and what do you think we've decided to do?"

"I haven't a clue."

"We're going to install a secret, home-made burglar alarm. Stagg worked out all the details, of course, but I don't mind admitting it was me who suggested it in the first place." Alfie breathed on his fingernails and polished them on the lapel of his jacket, which is the Sheldrakian way of showing that you're feeling pretty pleased with yourself.

A *secret* burglar alarm? An obvious flaw in the Stagg-Cutworth brainwave occurred to me, straight away. "But how can a burglar alarm be secret? Gadgets of that calibre ring bells and kick up no end of a hoo-hah!"

"Ah! *This* one doesn't. It flashes lights instead! Old Stagg has brought all the kit with him, and he's going to fix it up in the corridor during mid-morning break."

"Isn't that leaving it a bit late?" I objected. "Supposing Spikey gets busy before then."

Alfie shook his head knowingly. "He won't do that. There'll be P.E. classes going on outside on the games field for the first two lessons, and he'd never be able to get past them without being spotted. *After* break is the danger period—you mark my words." He spoke with the quiet confidence of one who has checked his facts and knows what he's talking about. . . . Without doubt, we could put our trust in A. Cutforth and fear naught.

In any case, further discussion was out of the question, because it was time for Assembly. So I parked my bike and went indoors to get ready for the day's labours.

The first two lessons dragged out their weary length, and at last the bell sounded for mid-morning break. Jigger and I followed our usual routine of tottering along to the dining-hall together to do a spot of much-needed refuelling on buns and milk; then we strolled back along the corridor leading past Form 4 classroom.

Here we found J. O. Stagg, heaven's gift to science, perched on top of the lockers and hard at work on the finishing stages of his latest invention. Alfie was assisting, of course; while Boko Phipps and Scuttersthorp, plus a few other spectators, were watching the proceedings with close attention.

"Roll up and see the famous demonstration," Boko greeted us. "There's been nothing to equal this since Watt invented the steam engine."

We examined the Staggers' latest engineering feat with keen interest. He had installed a high-tension wireless battery inside Jigger's locker and connected it to the catch on the locker door. Lengths of frayed flex protruded through a small hole in the back of the locker, and led up the wall and through the glass ventilator above our classroom door.

"After that it runs down the door-frame and along the skirting-board till it comes to my desk. Then it pips inside, *via* the inkwell, and joins on to a light bulb hidden behind my textbooks," the inventor explained proudly.

"I'll take your word for it," I said. "But I still don't see what it *does*."

"I should have thought it was obvious. Anyone opening Jigger's locker makes a connection with the wireless battery, which switches the light on inside my desk. All I've got to do is to take a squint under the lid every so often, and I'll know at once if anyone's messing about with the locker out here in the corridor"

It sounded simple enough in theory. In practice, however, snags arose owing to the inventor's lack of decent equipment. For instance, the numerous short pieces of flex which he was patiently joining together were so ancient and decayed that odd strands of bare wire kept peeping through the perished rubber covering. This didn't seem to worry him though; neither did the fact that the bits and pieces he was trailing up the wall passed uncomfortably close to something that looked like a strip of wire running the length of the corridor high up above the lockers.

For a moment this had me guessing. I'd seen the wire-strip dozens of times before, but offhand I couldn't think what it was. I stood brooding on this while the conversation flowed on about me.

"Yes, that's all very well," Boko was saying. "But even if this chronic contraption *does* work, what happens then? We can't all charge out in the middle of maths just because Spikey's up to a spot of no-good on the other side of the door!"

The Staggers hadn't thought of that. He was so

bowled over by the brilliance of his famous invention that he hadn't spared a thought for what was going to happen in the later stages of the proceedings.

"Oh, we'll think of something," he called down airily from his lofty perch. "Perhaps I could signal to Milligan when the light goes on; and then we could—er—well, he could pretend to come over all faint, and Johnson could escort him up to the sick room."

"And as soon as they get outside the door they can pounce on Spikey and shut him up in the boot-room till after school," Cutforth suggested brightly.

Well, I ask you! Did you ever hear such a bat-witted idea in your life? But that's Messrs Cutforth and Stagg all over. So long as *their* part of the scheme worked according to schedule, somebody else could tackle the sticky end of the job when the fateful moment arrived.

"It'd never work in a million years," said Jigger, shaking his head sorrowfully. "Far better take the whole contraption down and just trust to luck. Besides, I don't think this gadget is safe with all these bits of frayed flex trailing about the place. You'll probably get a short circuit and give yourself an electric shock every time you open your desk lid."

Boko nodded in agreement. "Hear, hear! This wheeze is a wash-out. In any case, Spikey may not come at all. We can't even be certain that he knows where to find the flag if he *does* come."

"He knows all right—*and* he'll come for it. It's all fixed," Alfie Cutforth replied in confident tones. "I had my ears pretty well out on strings when Bubble-gum was letting the cat out of the bag. I've got their little scheme well taped, don't you worry."

It was then that I remembered what the strip of wire was for.

"I say, Staggers, you want to be careful of that," I told him. "It's part of the automatic fire alarm. That's the wire that snaps and sets the bell going when the place gets too hot."

"Oh, is it? Well, I shan't hurt it. I'll keep my flex out of the way, if poss." Whereupon the inventor arranged his bits of tattered wiring so that they crossed the automatic alarm at right-angles. Whether or not they were actually touching it I couldn't see from down below. I could only keep my fingers crossed and hope for the best, as Stagg put the finishing touches to his handiwork and said: "There, that's got everything fixed. All I've got to do now is to test it out and see how it goes."

But there was no time to test it out, for as he finished speaking and jumped down from the lockers, the bell rang for the end of break. Almost immediately afterwards Mr. Birkinshaw, our form master, came striding along the corridor and chivvied us into class without more ado.

"Oh, fish-hooks! What a bind! Well, I suppose I'll just have to chance it," I heard Stagg mutter, as he made for his desk.

We hurried to our places and scavenged in our desk for pens, books and blotting paper. The lesson was history: and that morning the routine consisted of taking down notes, rattled by Old Birkie at wrist-aching speed. He started dictating almost before he got inside the door and went on at a lively pace for nearly twenty minutes; during which time no sound was heard apart from Mr. Birkinshaw's honeyed tones and the clicking of crossed nibs trying to keep up with the flow of knowledge.

And then it happened!

At precisely 11.37 a.m. by our classroom clock, the

orderly calm was shattered by the raucous, ear-splitting shrilling of the automatic fire alarm.

Nervous types jumped like startled deer; pens leaped from quivering fingers, and carefully balanced ink-pots rocked on their pivots and turned turtle, as the nervous jumpers reacted violently to the sudden shock.

You see, our fire alarm makes a noise like something from another world, and it's quite the most fearsome racket that has even fallen upon the human ear. It combines the shriek of an atomic rocket with the clatter of an iron foundry—the sort of sound that fastens itself to your ear-drums and won't let go.

"Fire drill," announced Mr. Birkinshaw, in case we hadn't guessed. At least, his lips framed the words, but we couldn't hear him above the noise of the alarm.

Obediently we closed all the windows, and got into line ready to march outside on to the quad. The clanging ceased as we were about to move off.

"Please, sir, is it a practice or the real thing, sir?" asked Alfie Cutforth.

"Silence! No talking during fire drill," retorted Mr. Birkinshaw. "Lead on, Johnson. . . . No overtaking, and no hurrying in the corridor!"

I had a pretty shrewd idea that I could have answered Alfie's question for him. My guess was that it wasn't a practice and it wasn't a fire—it was gimcrack workmanship on the part of Stagg that had set the alarm going by accident.

I wanted to be sure of this, so I managed to be the last one to leave the classroom—apart from Old Birkie, of course—and as soon as I had gone through the door my fears were confirmed. The automatic fire alarm wire had snapped at the point where Stagg's shaggy bits of flex had crossed it at right-angles. What's more, it was obvious that they had not only crossed it, but had been touching it, causing a nasty short circuit to warm up the wire for twenty minutes with current kindly supplied by the wireless battery.

All things considered, it seemed as though the inventor would find himself batting on a sticky wicket if the H.M. should start making inquiries when once the excitement was over. . . . Something would have to be done!

Mr. Birkinshaw had followed me into the corridor, but now he hastened along towards the head of the file to pounce on some ill-disciplined specimen who was nattering to his neighbour. Here was my chance to remove the tell-tale evidence!

I made a quick grab at Stagg's dangling piece of flex. They came away in half a dozen short lengths and dropped down out of sight behind the lockers. There was now no trace of Staggers' handiwork to be seen, so I hurried forward and caught up with the tail-end of my form as they rounded the bend of the corridor.

By now the building was alive with boys. Landings, stairways and passages resounded to the tread of sturdy teenage footwear as class after class came streaming out of their form-rooms and made their way outside on to the quad in accordance with the fire-drill regulations.

Quite by accident the Staggers had started things moving in a big way. . . . Still, it made a pleasant change from copying down Old Birkie's history notes!

FINAL RECKONING

FIRE drill at Sheldrake's is a sight well worth watching. Six hundred boys and thirty-odd masters march to their roll-call positions with the precision of a brigade of infantry at a royal review. Then the school lines up in two long ranks, facing each other and stretching from the gates right across the quad to the main doors, where the Head-hunter stands to await reports that everyone is out of the building.

Well, this drill went according to plan. The check-up showed that nobody was missing, and that the building wasn't on fire anyway.

All this took a little time to organize, but when at last the Head was satisfied, he ran his eye along the ranks of boys ranged before him and spake thus: "I should, perhaps, tell you that our fire drill this morning was not arranged intentionally. It appears that some electrical fault developed in the automatic system, which had the effect of sounding the alarm unexpectedly. However, this has given us a further opportunity to practise our fire drill, and I am more than satisfied with the way in which it has been carried out."

I think he would have said a good deal more, but at that moment a diversion occurred. A figure turned in through the school gates, and gave a little start of surprise at the sight of the six hundred boys lining the route like a guard of honour. The visitor was a tall, thin, elderly character, wearing a cloth cap, a hairy tweed suit and gold-rimmed bi-focal spectacles.

Dr. Stallybone! . . . Gosh! And I had forgotten to tell the Head that he was coming!

For two seconds the worthy doctor stood staring at the assembled school in some bewilderment. Then he drew himself erect, and started to tread the long aisle between the guard of honour, bowing left and right like royalty acknowledging the homage of the multitude. Only too clearly I could guess what was going on in his mind. He must have thought that the whole six hundred of us, plus staff, had turned out and lined the route specially to welcome him!

On he walked, trying to look calm and dignified, while at the same time bursting with pleasure and pride at the honour that was being accorded him. At last he reached the broad steps of the main entrance. He paused to survey the figures of the masters, as though tossing up in his mind which one must be the Head.

His guess turned out to be right! He trotted forward to greet Mr. Hunter with a bashful smile and outstretched hand.

"How do you do, Headmaster. I am delighted to meet you!" he twittered. "I am deeply honoured by this cordial reception—deeply honoured, I assure you. When I sent word that I was coming I did not, of course, mean to imply that my visit should be regarded as a formal occasion. However, it is most gratifying to be given such an enthusiastic welcome—most gratifying indeed!"

The Head-hunter was nonplussed. However, he rallied gamely and did his best to cope with the unexpected turn of events. He shook hands and smiled to conceal the fact that he hadn't a clue who the visitor was, or what he had come for. Politely he murmured: "I am so pleased you were able to come, Mr.—er—um . . ."

"Stallybone. Dr. Stallybone."

"Ah, yes, of course. Dr. Stallybone, to be sure."

I was near enough to hear both sides of the conversation, and to observe that the Head was racking his brains like blinko.

"Let me see now, Dr. Stallybone. You have come along to—er—to . . . ?"

"To make my donation to the Great Hall Fund. As I told the boys who called to return my notes the other evening, I should be only too pleased to contribute the sum of—of . . ."

Dr. Stallybone hesitated. *One* pound had been the amount that he had had in mind when we'd called at his house the previous Saturday; but now he was so overwhelmed at his magnificent reception that he hardly liked to suggest such a paltry sum. So, flushed with pride, and throwing caution to the winds, he blurted out: "I should be delighted to make a donation of *five* pounds."

I couldn't help smiling while the Head was making his speech of thanks. Little did the generous donor know that the impressive guard of honour was not intended for him at all. . . . And little did the Head-hunter know that if it hadn't been for the fire drill we should never have had that extra four pounds!

Just as the H.M. finished his oration, Dr. Stallybone caught sight of Jigger and me standing smartly to attention in our places. At once his face lit up in recognition.

"Why, those are the boys who inspired my modest contribution," he told the H.M. "They went to a great deal of trouble to find an important bird-watching manuscript which I had carelessly mislaid. I am more grateful to them than I can say."

The Head switched on his most human smile.

"Milligan and Johnson, eh? Splendid! They have

already set a good example by organizing a jumble sale which resulted in a very satisfactory sum being added to the Great Hall Fund. And now, with this handsome donation of yours, Doctor, to add to their credit they will have been responsible for raising—well Johnson, what is the total?"

"Twenty-nine pounds, eighty-five and a half pence, sir, said Jigger, doing complicated calculations on his fingers.

The Head nodded approvingly, and turned again to his guest. "Our efforts to raise the money for our Great Hall have had the most encouraging results," he explained. "Every form in the school has responded magnificently. And with the addition of your generous gift, I think it is safe to say that we have reached the target we set ourselves. Furthermore, I shall announce to the school at assembly tomorrow that the work of restoring our Hall will be put in hand without delay."

After that he dismissed the fire-drill parade and led the way indoors to his study. At his heels trotted Dr. Stallybone, with fountain-pen poised and cheque-book held at the ready.

"It's a pity we didn't quite manage to raise the thirty pounds, Rex," Jigger said to me as we came out on to the quad when school was over that afternoon. "Of course, twenty-nine pounds odd is a pretty good effort, but it still gives Alfie a chance to say we didn't reach the target."

"M'yes," I agreed. "Though don't forget the Head hasn't made the announcement yet. D'you think we could raise the odd pence before assembly tomorrow morning?"

Jigger shook his head. "Not unless we give it out of our own pockets—and *that* doesn't really count. If you remember, we decided that the contributions must either be earned or subscribed by somebody outside the school."

Just then J. O. Stagg rounded the corner of the gymnasium, pushing his bicycle and balancing the ill-fated wireless battery on the handlebars.

"All my trouble for nothing," he moaned as he came up to us. "I spent hours working on that burglar alarm, and then we couldn't use it after all."

"It was a pretty ribby effort, if you ask me," said Jigger. "And what's more, it was jolly lucky for you that Rex covered up your traces. The Head would have had a few things to say if he knew what had *really* started the fire-bell going."

"Oh, that was just a bit of bad luck—the sort of thing that might happen to anyone," the inventor replied. His face clouded over with frustration as he went on: "What gets me down is that I went to all the trouble of rigging up that apparatus to catch Spikey Andrews, and then the chap hadn't got the decency to turn up!"

"I don't blame him. Anyone with any sense would keep as far away from your lethal gadgets as they possibly could!"

I glanced round as I spoke; and then gave a whistle of surprise as, for the second time that day, I caught sight of an unexpected guest turning in through the school gates.

"Wow! Here *is* Spikey after all," I gasped. "Marching in the front way, too, as though he belonged to the place."

"Gosh, what cheek!" fumed Jigger. "And he's even had the sauce to bring that ghastly Bubblegum specimen with him too!"

"Better late than never," I said. "But I wonder what

his idea is! He can't be after our flag, or he'd have tried to sneak in the back way."

The leader of the Tech Brigade, followed by his toothy henchman, advanced towards us across the quad. There was nothing furtive about his movements, either.

"Hullo, Spikey. What are you doing here?" I greeted him.

The usual grin spread slowly across the Andrews countenance from east to west.

"Hullo, Milligan. We've brought something for you. At least, it isn't for *you*, it's for this moth-eaten old dump of yours." He jerked his thumb in the direction of the Great Hall and handed me a screw of newspaper containing twenty-seven pence.

"It's a sort of surprise that Spikey and me planned over the week-end," volunteered Bubblegum.

Jigger and I were dumbfounded. We just couldn't believe that the Tech Brigade could entertain such tender feelings on our behalf.

"Yes, but look here—I mean . . . Well, it's jolly decent of you, but we couldn't possibly accept it—thanks all the same," I faltered.

"Why not? We're not *giving* you anything—we're just paying off an old debt," Spikey answered. He saw my look of bewilderment and went on: "We heard you chaps had been put to a bit of expense over the cleaning job you did at Old Snorker's house. We got a jolly good laugh out of that caper, so we thought it only fair to subscribe something towards it."

"But where did you get the money from?" asked Jigger, still feeling a little dazed.

"We earned it," said Bubblegum proudly. "Spikey and I went round to Elm Gardens yesterday evening and did three hours' baby-minding for Old Snorker and his wife."

Spikey turned on his henchman with some heat.

"You needn't go about telling everyone, you flat-footed bazooka," he stormed. "Why can't you keep your big trap shut? A nice sort of clodpoll I'll look up at the Tech if the story gets around that I've been baby-sitting."

Then his indignation faded and he turned to me with his usual broad grin. "Well, cheerio, Milligan. See you on the battlefield, eh? What about a return skirmish next Saturday?"

"Suits me," I agreed.

"Right-O, then. Same time and place—and no garden rollers this time, eh! . . . Come on, Bubblegum, get mobile, you ancient relic."

He gave his friend a quick left-and-right to the body and a snappy upper-cut to the jaw, just to show there was no ill-feeling. Then the pair of them wandered off towards the road.

"Well, well! So Spikey did come after all! And not to pull a fast one on us, either," mused Jigger. "You wouldn't think, to look at him, that he's the sort of chap who goes about doing good by stealth, would you?"

I felt too dazed to do anything but nod in agreement. It was a shock to learn that our old enemy had such a friendly side to his nature. The very thought of the tough, ruthless dictator of the Tech Brigade actually *baby-minding* to help his deadly rivals out of a hole was enough to make the imagination boggle in bewilderment. . . . And what made his generous gesture even more worthwhile was the fact that his twenty-seven pence sent our roof-raising collection soaring over the thirty-pound mark—just!

The Staggers had been gazing dreamily into space while we'd been talking to Spikey; but now he pulled himself together and said in his rich, plummy accents: "I'm glad they want another battle. I shall have to look slippy with my secret weapon, though, if its got to be ready by Saturday."

"What secret weapon are you woffling about?" queried Jigger.

"Why, the one I'm inventing for our next skirmish with the Tech," Stagg explained. "Didn't I tell you? It's a sort of trench-mortar that sends gas-filled bladders sailing through the air to land behind the enemy lines. Or you could use it against their infantry as they charge into the attack if you want to."

Jigger tapped his forehead pityingly and clicked his teeth in despair. I kept a straight face and did my best to humour the man of science.

"It sounds a pretty fearsome weapon," I agreed. "Though it may be just a *leetle* unreliable if it's anything like the rest of your patent gadgets."

"Oh, *this* one will work, don't you worry!" Stagg frowned with importance. "I would have got it finished a week ago, only I had a bit of bad luck and had to stop production. You see, I lost the formula I made up for working out how much gas the football bladders would take without bursting."

"Yes, I can quite see that would be a . . . WHAT!!"

I broke off and leapt as though I'd been stung, as the meaning of his words touched off a fuse in my slow-working brain.

"*Formula!* What was that you said about a formula?" I shouted, waving my arms like a paddle-steamer out of control, and hopping from foot to foot in feverish agitation.

Stagg opened his eyes wide in surprise, and stepped back out of range of my wildly-flailing arms.

"I only said I made one up," he defended himself. "Unfortunately I lost it. I must have left it in that despatch case I had my eye on at the jumble sale, but I didn't remember about it till afterwards, and by that time somebody had bought it."

The landscape rocked before my eyes. I clasped my hand to my brow and tottered round in small circles.

"You mean to say *you made it up*?" I gasped when I had ceased revolving. "You mean to stand there and tell me that all that gobbledeygook about Admin. Room M/47 and 'H' Group Research Personnel was just a lot of shatterpated moonshine?"

The Staggers looked puzzled. "How did you know about the *ATIR* scheme?" he demanded.

"Never mind how we know, you shrimp-witted problem child! What on earth possessed you to type out all that dehydrated balderdash in the first place?"

The inventor looked a trifle sheepish. "Well, all decent scientists have a formula when they're working on important stuff like secret weapons," he confessed. "Mind you, the *ATIR* scheme wasn't what you could call a proper formula—or rather it didn't really *mean* anything—but it was jolly useful, all the same!"

"Useful?" echoed Jigger weakly.

"Oh, yes! It helped create the right sort of scientific atmosphere, which is so important when you're engaged in hush-hush work of this type."

There was a short silence. Then Jigger heaved a long-drawn sigh like an electric train applying its vacuum brakes. At last he said: "Oh, well, I suppose we ought to have guessed."

I nodded. It wasn't the first time that the inventive genius of J. O. Stagg had led us up the garden. It's all very well for *him* to live in the make-believe world of his own imagination; but it's a little hard on the rest of us who have to put up with the consequences.

"You don't happen to know what's become of the formula, do you?" Stagg inquired earnestly. "I'd like to get it back, if poss. It's jolly difficult constructing the prototype of a new sort of trench-mortar without any notes to refer to."

Into my mind's eye there flashed the sudden vision of our long-suffering police sergeant. By this time he would have made his inquiries and found out for himself that he had been on a wild goose chase. He might even think that we had concocted the scheme on purpose; in which case it would be as well to steer clear of the danger area until his sarcastic comments had cooled off to something below sizzling point.

"Well, if you really *must* have your precious document back, you'll have to ask the sergeant at Marlborough Road police station," I said. "But I warn you; his remarks about bogus atomic formulae are liable to be a trifle terse."

"Oh, I'll risk that," smiled the wonder-man of science, squeezing the wireless battery into his saddlebag. "I'll tell him about a new idea I'm working on for photographing the footprints of cat-burglars in foggy weather. That ought to put him in a decent mood if he's keen on his job."

He swung his leg over the saddle and pedalled off on his dangerous mission. As we watched him go I couldn't help wondering what sort of reception he'd get when he waltzed into the police station to claim his property. I wasn't really worried, though. People seldom get in much of a bate with well-meaning clodpolls like old Staggers.

The quad was almost deserted by now, for it was

well past our usual time for going home. Most of the chaps had already left; but before we could follow their example, Jigger and I had one last job to do. . . . We took Spikey's twenty-seven p along to the Head-hunter's study and made our final contribution to the roof-raising fund.

Then we retrieved our bikes and set off together on the homeward trek. We were just turning out of the school gates when Jigger glanced back at the Great Hall on the far side of the quad. "I'm glad we reached our target," he remarked. "Now it's all over I don't mind telling you there were times when I thought we'd never do it."

I nodded in agreement. The task hadn't been easy, but it had been great fun. And as we pedalled along the road my mind drifted back over the more hair-raising exploits of the past few weeks. I thought of the fiasco at Elm Gardens, the panic at the cycle track, the chaos at the jumble sale. I thought of innocent refugees, of inoffensive bird-watchers, of gimcrack burglar alarms and gas-filled football bladders. . . . And I thought of our battles with the Tech and the change of heart that had come upon our old foe Spikey Andrews.

Jigger must have been thinking along the same lines, because when we reached the turning to his road he didn't swerve off as he usually does. Instead, he put his foot down on the kerb and sat staring into the middle distance, a wan smile hovering round the corners of his mouth. Clearly, some great meditation was brewing in the brain of J. I. G. Johnson.

"What's up?" I asked.

"Nothing. I was only thinking," he replied, coming out of his trance. "I was just thinking how some people managed to go through life without dropping bricks all over the place, and finding themselves in trouble up to the eyebrows. . . . But not you and me! *Not* Messrs. Milligan and Johnson—oh, no!"

He shook his head sadly; but all the same there was a gleam of laughter in his eyes as he turned to me and added: Honestly, Rex—the things that happen to us! You could almost write a book about them."

Write a book about them!

"I say, that's not a bad scheme, Jig," I answered as the idea took shape in my mind. "Yes, I think I will!"

And, what's more, I *have*!

Coming in Armada

February 1974

The Hardy Boys Adventure Series

The Mystery of the Aztec Warrior

The Arctic Patrol Mystery

The Haunted Fort

The Mystery of the Whale Tattoo

Price 25p